Praise for Reinve

"*Reinventing Yourself* is written forcefully, but with great humor, There won't be many books in the coming years that are met with as much enthusiasm as his book."

—Colin Wilson, author of *The Outsider and Alien Dawn*

"If you want a book that develops your hidden potential, look no further, Steve Chandler's *Reinventing Yourself* is it!"

—Danny Cox, author of *Seize the Day* and

There are No Limits

20TH ANNIVERSARY EDITION

Reinventing Yourself

How to Become the Person You've Always Wanted to Be

Steve Chandler

CAREER PRESS

This edition first published in 2017 by Career Press, an imprint of
Red Wheel/Weiser, LLC
With offices at:
65 Parker Street, Suite 7
Newburyport, MA 01950
www.redwheelweiser.com
www.careerpress.com

ISBN: 978-1-63265-090-0
Library of Congress Cataloging-in-Publication Data available
upon request.

Cover design by Howard Grossman/12E Design
Interior by PerfecType, Nashville, TN

Printed in the United States of America
IBI
10 9 8 7 6 5 4 3 2 1

CONTENTS

FOREWORD

The story of who I was . . . was just a story

When I was in fourth grade, a bunch of girls passed around a note telling people not to be my friend, which started years of being teased and bullied. I made that mean I was unlikable.

At 10 years old, I was diagnosed with depression, put on Prozac, and told I had a "chemical imbalance" that I would need to be medicated for just like a diabetic would take insulin. I made that mean I was broken.

During my teenage years I had a series of unrequited crushes and lack of friends. I made that mean that I was alone and not desirable.

Throughout school I was a straight-A student, always at the top of the class. My teachers gave me lots of validation for that. My parents were very proud of me. And everyone told me that I would be very successful. I made that mean that my sense of worth came from my intelligence and what I could achieve.

All these things started forming the story of who I was, and I made choices that supported that story. Since I believed on some level that I was unlikable, broken, and undesirable, and that my worth came from achieving, I became addicted to being the best. I was incredibly driven. It is truly amazing how feeling like you have something to prove to the world will drive you.

By the age of 25, I was the youngest female agent in the highly competitive field of Hollywood. I was making money, going to all the best parties and events, and hob-knobbing with celebrities. Not to mention making a great salary for someone just a few years out of college.

There was just one problem: The same "me" was still there no matter how much money I made, whom I dated, or what external goal I could accomplish. And I really didn't like the "me" that I was. My drive came with intense self-criticism. My "I-have-it-all-together" exterior masked massive insecurity.

And I kept hoping that something or someone outside of me would occur that would finally provide me with the fulfillment, peace of mind, happiness, and love that I craved.

But that didn't exactly happen. . . .

Everything came crashing down around me at 26 when in a span of eight months I resigned from my fancy career because I just could not take the stress anymore, but it only threw me into a deeper depression because my role as a successful agent had become my identity and source of self-worth. Then I went into massive debt, got diagnosed with an un-diagnosable auto-immune disorder on top of the depression I was still on medication for, and also became suddenly estranged from my family. But the one thing I clung onto was my fiancé. He was the answer!!! He was my salvation!! Sure, I had lost a lot but now I was going to be a wife. Great! That could be my new identity. And this was reassuring until six months before our wedding he dumped me cold turkey.

I felt like a total victim. One night I sought comfort on my cold tiles of my bathroom floor asking, "Why is this happening *to* me??" When I heard myself ask that question it suddenly dawned on me . . . . *Wait a second. I am the common denominator in all of these situations. So if I had something to do with creating them, perhaps I have influence on how to change them.*

And that is when my life shifted from one of a victim to one of an owner. I stopped asking "Why is this happening *to* me?" and started asking "Why is this happening *for* me? What can I learn and how can I shift it?" As I started asking those questions, I began the process of reinventing myself. Dropping the old stories that were holding me back and creating similar undesirable events in my life. I began to take responsibility for myself. Instead of feeling sorry for myself, I began to change my beliefs about myself and life in general.

Consequently, my entire life did change. Today I experience those feelings of fulfillment, peace of mind, happiness, and love that I craved because I generate them from the inside. I have been off anti-depressants for nearly a decade and do work in the world that I absolutely love. I have an amazing connection with my family and a group of friends that I call my "soul family."

I am not special. I have no super powers. I just realized that the most powerful choice we have is how we define ourselves.

Since this book has landed in your lap, that is the powerful choice that is in front of you right now.

How do you want to define yourself?

Do you want to continue to believe an old story about yourself? Do you want to continue to wait for someone else to change or someone to come along on a white horse and save you from yourself? Do you want to continue to blame your parents or society for why you don't have what you want? Do you want to continue to believe that it's too late or too hard to go after your dreams?

Even if you are tempted a tiny little bit to say yes to anything of those things, Steve Chandler will lead you to take charge of your life in this book by shifting from victim to owner. He will inspire you to reinvent yourself and show you that it's actually not as hard as you think (or as you've been making it).

I hired Steve as my coach three years ago and he challenged me to get out of my comfort zone in terms of my business. In just one month, he helped me change my entire business model. He saw that I was playing too small and reminded me of a possibility that was more powerful than my fear of making changes. Sure, I was scared, but Steve reminded me that courage is not the absence of fear, rather it is feeling the fear and moving forward anyway.

And Steve will do the same for you in this book. In his strong and playful way, he will shine a light on the blind spots that are keeping you stuck in an old paradigm. He will teach you how to truly see yourself and the power you have over your own life.

Get ready because it is time for you to stop playing small. It is time for you to get out of that old, comfy story about who you are. It is time for you to be a loving leader in your relationships and career. It is time for you to go after those dreams and goals that you have been too afraid to pursue. It is time for you to free yourself from the prison of a constructed identity that is not true.

It is time for you to reinvent yourself!

Christine Hassler
Author of *Expectation Hangover*

Part One

● ● ●

Owners of the Spirit

Spirit—(spir' it) n. 1. The vital principle or animating force within living beings.

—*The American Heritage Dictionary*

1

Remove Your Ball
and Chain

IN ORDER FOR US TO learn how to be owners of the human spirit, it helps if we know what being an owner looks and feels like. It helps to have a picture.

I remember a few years ago when I gave two of my daughters a picture.

Margie and Stephanie were both rehearsing for school singing assignments. Margie was in sixth grade, singing a school choir solo of a song from *Beauty and the Beast*, and Stephanie was rehearsing for the junior high school talent show, in which she was going to sing a Mariah Carey song called "Hero."

Both girls asked me to listen to their rehearsals. I did, and I told them that they sounded good enough musically. Both girls had good voices and were hitting the notes, but something was missing: the spirit—the vital principle—the animating force.

I told them it was okay to let loose a little, to really get into it. I recommended that they start to over-rehearse, to rehearse enough times to reach a state of *ownership* of the song. To get that feeling that the song was all theirs, flowing out of them naturally, powerfully.

Margie pinned a piece of paper to the wall of her bedroom and made a mark on it every time she sang her song. She sang it over, and over, and over.

Stephanie also rehearsed more and more, and still her song was coming out tentative and prissy, held way back.

But they both pushed on.

Finally, Margie's concert came and she was great. She stood out when her solo came because she sang with fire and force, whereas the other girls and boys that night were like little cautious robots. The extra rehearsals had given Margie ownership.

Next up was Stephanie's talent show, and things still weren't right with her song. Her rehearsals still weren't taking her performance anywhere.

So I got an idea. I went to a video store and found a used copy of a musical documentary of Janis Joplin's life. It contained a concert performance that I had been lucky enough to be present at: her performance at Monterey Pop Festival with her band Big Brother and The Holding Company.

At the time of the concert, I was stationed at the Presidio of Monterey in the U.S. Army. I was there that late afternoon sitting by myself in a fourth-row seat when Janis blew a hole in the music world with her performance of "Ball and Chain." The moment is also captured in the film *Monterey Pop*, with Mama Cass Elliot in the same audience shown in a reaction shot to Janis Joplin, her mouth gaping in awe.

Janis Joplin was on fire that day. I never saw anything like it. None of today's feisty, angry female rockers quite have the exact spirit, because Janis wasn't as angry as she was, well, on fire.

I put the videotape in for Stephanie and Margie to watch, and I'd cued it up to the performance of "Ball and Chain." We watched together, and as usual, I got goose bumps and tears in my eyes as I watched.

I got that same feeling I always get when I see the ownership of spirit. I got it when I saw the early, young Elvis. I used to get it watching a lyrically insane football player named Chuck Cecil play football. I've gotten it watching Michael Jordan play basketball with the flu and still outplay the whole court. Or watching Alvin Lee and Ten Years After at Woodstock. I've gotten it watching Pavarotti sing "Nessum Dorma" and almost explode with the joy and volume of the song. I've gotten it watching Marlon Brando in *One-Eyed Jacks* and Jack Nicholson in *A Few Good Men*. I've gotten it hearing Buffy Ste. Marie sing "God Is Alive, Magic Is Afoot" from Leonard Cohen's *Beautiful Losers*. When you're in the presence of an owner of the spirit, you know the feeling.

Owners of the spirit *are* beautiful losers. They risk all. They are losers because they have lost all fear of embarrassment. They have lost all inhibition. They have lost all concern for what other people might think.

Stephanie's eyes grew a little wider as Janis Joplin sang on. The passion and abandon and power in that one small woman was something that only a corpse would be unmoved by. When the song was over, the video showed Mama Cass mouthing the word "wow" just as Stephanie said the same thing.

And a hero comes along

While I was putting the tape away, I told Stephanie, "There are times in life when you know you have a chance to really go for it. You are a great singer, so I know you're going to sing your song very well in the show. You have to decide for yourself how much you're going to go for it. You are never who you think you are. You can be anyone you want. When you're singing, you might remember Janis Joplin."

The night of the talent show was fun and lighthearted. I had all but forgotten about my Janis Joplin lecture with Stephanie, and I was just there to enjoy the show and see her sing.

After a few acts in which the performers showed varying degrees of talent and self-consciousness, it was Stephanie's turn. She had a compact disc of the background music and background vocals to the song "Hero" and she stepped out on stage in a black dress and began the song as her friends in the audience in the gym cheered and clapped to encourage her.

Her voice was a little weak and nervous at the start, although right on pitch as she softly sang through the first verse, looking out at the crowd and occasionally smiling with self-consciousness. As her song continued to build, I saw something start to change in Stephanie. She stomped her high-heeled shoe forward as the song took the turn into the last verse and she was no longer smiling. Her voice grew louder and louder and you could tell that the audience no longer existed for her. It was just the song. Tears welled up in my eyes and I could feel my heart race and my throat tighten, and I remember thinking, "She's going for it. She's going for it."

Stephanie rounded the corner into the last chorus in full possession of the song, sending it through her spirit and out into the auditorium in a way that I'd never heard her sing before. The kids in the audience jumped to their feet and raised their hands and started screaming, but Stephanie's voice soared beyond them, above it all, living only for itself as the song came to an end among the loudest sustained cheers of the evening.

Even grownups were on their feet at the end, knowing that they had just lived a moment they themselves may not have seen in a long while—a moment of the human spirit on fire.

I turned to my friends and family and said, "Wow." I was inspired. I'd shown Stephanie Janis Joplin, and then Stephanie showed me Stephanie.

The trick is to pass it on.

The song of the hero is in you

Oliver Wendell Holmes observed, "Most people go to their graves with their music still in them." He was right; most people do. But that's because they've never heard that music. They simply don't know it's there.

There was nothing in the circumstance itself that caused Stephanie to find her spirit. The whole point of watching the Janis Joplin video was to show her that it can be invented.

You can tap into the spirit in yourself. Anytime you want. It's always there. Stephanie doesn't have anything that you don't have. Janis Joplin didn't have anything that Stephanie didn't have.

The next time you see the spirit in someone else, don't just admire it; think of how to do your own version of it. Don't envy it; duplicate it.

Talk to yourself. Start thinking about it. Practice saying, "I can do that!" every time you see someone do something great. Most people say, "Wow, I could never do that." They've built a deep neural pathway with that negative affirmation. By saying, "I could never do that," they deepen the illusion that they are stuck in something mediocre, that they are stuck in *someone* mediocre.

You can set yourself free by changing how you talk to yourself about your capabilities. The greatness you see in others is also in you. I promise you that you can find it inside you, no matter who you are, no matter who you've invented yourself to be.

Stephanie saw herself in Janis. You will see yourself in Stephanie. Someday I will see myself in you. The trick is to pass it on.

2

Life Is a Bitch and Then You Die?

A FEW YEARS AGO, I was watching a TV ad for Gatorade, and Michael Jordan ended the spot by saying, "Life is a sport . . . drink it up."

The commercial reminded me of a bumper sticker I've seen often over the years that says, "Life Is a Bitch and Then You Die." I have begun to use this bumper sticker as a teaching tool. It's one of the most effective tools I've ever used because of how quickly it reveals the key weakness in the victim's philosophy.

Not long ago I was conducting a workshop for a major high-tech company with about 100 people in the audience. As I wrote the words, "Life is a bitch and then you die," on the board, one of the participants called out, "Hey! I've got that on my coffee cup!"

"So . . . You drink from that philosophy every day?" I said.

"I guess I do," he said.

"Well, we're going to study it," I said. "When we're through, you might want to give that cup to someone you don't like."

The slogan "Life Is a Bitch and Then You Die" is a perfect expression of the core belief system of a victim. It also contains the key to why victimized thinking always leads to fatigue and low performance, and why victims are only victims of their own defeated thinking.

For the fun of it, let's say that the first half of the bumper sticker has some truth. Let's say that we agree that life is a bitch, or any variation of that: Life is difficult; life is unfair; life will wear you out; life is a struggle.

But if that is so, why is it so bad that "Then you die"? If life is so difficult, what's so negative about dying?

That's the contradiction. That's the double bind in the philosophy. It would be just like saying, "I hate being here, and what's worse is I might have to leave." Or, "I hate working here, and what's worse is that they might lay me off." Remarkably, a lot of people think exactly like that. About life, about their jobs, about their marriages, about everything. Like the singer in *Ol' Man River*: I'm "tired of livin' and scared of dyin'."

But the brain doesn't let us have it both ways. The human brain is a magical biocomputer. It sends us energy when we send it something clearly inspiring. But it slows us up when we feed it something that is self-contradictory. "Whoa!" shouts the chorus of cells in the brain and body. The brain and body go on strike against contradiction because the biocomputer wants harmonious logic. It always seeks out wholeness and completion.

It is *illogical* that life would be bad *and* death would be bad. In fact, if life *were* truly a bitch, then the bumper sticker ought to say, cheerfully, "Life is a bitch, *but* then you die!" Maybe put on a little happy face at the end. And then it might even help people more by putting a phone number at the bottom of the bumper sticker: "1-800-Kevorkian." It could be a service.

3

Astonishing Human Creations

SPIRIT IS A LOW FLAME inside us just waiting for the pump to bring the oxygen in. Outside circumstances do not activate the pump. We do. We can pump it anytime we want.

That's why taking a deep breath always improves any circumstance we are in. It dilutes fear and it focuses the mind. It relaxes the body and expands thinking, so it feeds the spirit. The word "inspire" literally means to "breathe in."

But if we never do this, the spirit will suffocate. The spirit will die inside a finished, stagnant personality. It can't breathe inside a sealed-off notion of who we are and always will be. Inside a cocoon.

As a child, I had terrible asthma (a disease characterized by an inability to breathe). I used to have a recurring dream almost every night that I was trying to shout back to my father who had accused me of something, and I couldn't speak, I couldn't breathe enough to speak, and my words came out in a strangled whisper. I was suffocating. I was trapped inside the person I thought I was. I thought I was a coward. I was once told I was, and, of course, I believed it.

That's probably why Dr. Nathaniel Branden used to warn parents to be careful what they say to their children, because the children do believe whatever is said. Forever and ever. Parents are gods to their children; they are the ultimate in power and authority. If your parents say you are lazy, it is not just an opinion, *it's who you are.*

We can stay stuck inside a childhood self-concept forever. But we don't have to. Especially once we see it was just an internal invention to begin with, a scar grown over the pain. If we were to fully understand how the mind operates, permanent pessimistic personalities would become a thing of the past. We would always be like children on Christmas morning, opening the gift of a brand new possibility. A brand new self, every morning.

I am fortunate because, in my profession as a coach, I watch people reinvent themselves every day. I recently watched Phil, an upper-level manager at a major utility company, deliberately change the person he had been trapped in for almost 20 years. He did it by understanding that he *could*—and then making the effort. He never understood how to do that before. He never really knew that one could rise above this deadly myth called "me." He never realized what noted Japanese psychotherapist Shoma Morita meant when he said, "Effort is good fortune."

Today I am a consultant to Phil as I watch him run his team meetings. I see him make and keep his promises to his people. I am privileged to watch him and learn from him. He is an inspiring, humble, and powerful leader. He is the person he always wanted to be, and each week he learns to grow even further. His happiness is his growth.

People change; people become happy. Happiness becomes a thing to be mastered. This is what life coach Devers Branden means when she conducts her innovative workshops on *The Discipline of Happiness.*

Consider our multiple personalities

An immediate member of my family suffered from multiple personality disorder. Although to say that she "suffered from" it is like saying Georgia O'Keefe "suffered from" her paintings, or that Michelangelo "suffered from" the Sistine Chapel.

She was brutally abused when she was a little girl, sexually and physically. The history of her abuse, when it was finally revealed, was almost too much for me to hear. Then I saw pictures and I saw that it was even worse than I'd heard.

As with most people who have multiple personality disorder, she had been misdiagnosed for most of her life. It wasn't until she was in her 30s that the truth came out.

The personalities she had invented to cope with the abuse as a child were the most astonishing human creations I had ever seen. My heart raced and my skin jumped as different voices, different faces, different *people* came from the same body in front of me. When she was hospitalized and diagnosed, it was found that each personality that came forward had different EEG waves. Some had physical marks that others didn't. Some personalities had voices that were different. Some were the voices of children. And as I listened to her, I was stunned to hear that these voices did not sound like those of a grown woman imitating a child, they sounded like actual children's voices.

The human brain will astonish you when backed into a corner. As a biocomputer, it is bordering on the magical. It will grow scars over the pain and call them personalities. (Sound familiar? We've all done that!)

After our family went through the upsetting crisis of reacting to her early diagnosis and various attempts at treatment, I began losing my fear of what was happening and started feeling a deep sense of awe at what the human mind could create in an emergency.

When she was a little girl, trying to avoid having to endure more awful abuse than she could handle, she split off and created someone new. It was an advanced form of self-hypnosis. Soon, the splitting and inventing happened again and again, and when the brain got good at it, it did it for even minor crises.

For a multiple, that's when it gets out of control and, in an adult, becomes a "disorder." What was originally an achievement of survival ends up a frightening problem.

Fortunately for our family, this human miracle of survival made it back in the game of life. She became a living example of the hero's journey. Her life showed us that the trip to happiness can go on *no matter what the circumstances.*

It's also a little funny to me when someone insists that people can't change who they are. Really?

Watch when I hand you this baby

Multiple personalities are among the most dramatic examples of how powerful we humans really are. We can be anybody we want to be. We invent ourselves as we go, we just don't know it.

If I hand you a baby to hold, what happens to you? Your voice changes, your face changes, and your vocabulary changes right before my eyes in a way that's almost too weird to witness. Your face turns to rubber and you start cooing and talking in a tiny voice. Have you ever changed! If you can do it in small ways, you can do it in big ways.

The asthma I had as a boy eventually went away as I learned to breathe into my own peaceful center. It went away as I learned to stand up for myself and to *create myself* in my speaking. My view of myself as a coward occasionally would linger on, but in ever-diminishing circles, like a film run backwards of a pebble thrown into a pool. I was no longer stuck inside my old story of who I was. I learned that I could always put a new film in and start over.

So who do you really want to be?

Keep in mind that you are many people. You can be whoever you want to be, with practice. You have inside you still more astonishing human creations waiting to be made up.

One of the reasons people love going to the movies is that we can watch our favorite actors do the ultimate in human creativity: create another human. We come away from the theater saying, "Meryl Streep was amazing," or "Robert DeNiro was incredible," or "Matt Damon made me cry." We deeply admire what they accomplished. They created human "beings."

Personality does the opposite of that.

Personality freezes us in a safe and secure pattern of being that we probably finished making up somewhere in junior high school. Most of our "permanent" personality was shaped from fear: fear of embarrassment, fear of losing face, fear of appearing uncool.

Grown-ups also have a fear of appearing false or phony, which causes them to want to be consistently fake. But to expand who you are and be someone stronger and more alive than you were yesterday is not being false; it is being true. It's being true to your potential, and true to your spirit. Your spirit wants to fly. It does not want to die inside a lonely prison cell that you have called your permanent final self.

Realize that who you think you "are" won't always work for the challenge at hand. Celebrate that. There's nothing wrong with it. In fact, it's good news because you now get to create some energy that will be up to the occasion. Leave personality behind. Drop it altogether. Try to have it be just you and the dream interacting, with no made-up personality getting in the way.

When you start relaxing the grip you have on your permanent identity and see that you can be anyone, who you *want to be* will become a more important person than who you "are." That moment in your life will be a big one.

4

Set Yourself Free From "I Gotta Be Me"

To BREAK THROUGH THE MYTH of human personality is to achieve real joy. And it's something we all can do when we start to realize how much control we have over who we are.

My friend Janese Morter is someone who I first heard sing in a church. I was a guest of her pastor that Sunday, and Janese had just moved to Phoenix from Chicago. She had already recorded one Gospel record, and she has one of those voices that can lift a human heart.

In the past, whenever I could get her to, she would sing a song right before the lunch break in my Owner–Victim seminar. It's from Michael Jordan's movie *Space Jam* and it's appropriately called "I Believe I Can Fly." As she soars within the song, you can hear that Janese is not singing from any kind of personality, but rather from the human spirit itself. People who hear her feel their own spirits start to stir.

Do you believe you can fly? Surveys show that most people have had dreams of flying. Deep down inside, we suspect that we're not stuck here on the ground. Even though we often claim to be weary and "down," we secretly long for lives of pure and soaring action. It happens in dreams because our dream body knows what we really want. Jiminy Cricket and Freud were in agreement that a dream is a wish your heart makes. Your heart knows who you really are. You are an angel. And as it is so poetically presented in Willie Nelson's song, you are an "angel flying too close to the ground."

Lives of soaring action are described by action words. And it was Buckminster Fuller who first observed, "I seem to be a verb!" And in that one powerful observation, he expressed a valuable secret of human potential. Owners of the spirit *know* that they are verbs—pure action words. Victims remain convinced that they are nouns: things, permanent things.

But the thing called *personality* is merely an illusion. We can change it at will. For example, it is a different "me" that goes to answer the door when my children say, "Dad, some guy from the IRS is here to talk to you," than if they were to come in and say, "Dad, a woman named Jennifer Lopez is here to see you." It is a different "me," because what the victim calls *personality* is just a history of habits.

The extensive work done by Dr. Martin Seligman on learned optimism spanned 20 years, and he studied more than half a million children and adults. He found and scientifically confirmed two things: 1) Optimism makes you more effective at whatever you do, and 2) *optimism can be learned.*

These findings confirmed the work of many other great contemporary psychologists who have put to death all the old superstitions revolving around the fear that you can't teach an old dog new tricks. The truth is, you can. This old dog, for one, can tell you.

People who have figured out how to access and own this optimistic spirit soon become less interested in their personalities than they are in their purpose. They love designing commitments and keeping them. They see them as the basic building blocks of a happy life.

People who have *not* connected to this spirit do not have much interest in commitments, but instead retain an exaggerated fascination with their own put-upon identities.

The elevator ride up from hell

An owner will change his personality on the spot in order to keep a commitment. A victim will break any commitment in order to keep his personality.

When victims discuss commitment, they refer to it as a *feeling* that comes and goes, as in, "I don't feel as committed to this person as I used to." They will say, "I gotta be me," especially when you point out that they are breaking their promises to another. They want personality to trump commitment.

The misplaced loyalty we give to our personalities causes us tremendous misery and confusion throughout our lives.

A longtime friend of mine who is a talented musician and songwriter wrote to me after I'd sent him an audio version of my Owner–Victim seminar. His words are an illustration of how quickly someone can change once he sees the mistake in his original thinking. It is not about years of therapy and transformation; it is about an *understanding* that can be immediate:

> You clearly heard my last desperate cry from the wilderness and, like a red cross of the spirit, you

responded. . . . I spent an entire week in my office listening over and over to this voice that spoke directly
to the core of my being, teaching me much I needed
to know but didn't, and reminding me of much I've
known but "down I forgot as up I grew." Nothing had
a greater impact on me than the seminal wisdom of
the price we pay for the "I Gotta Be Me" orientation.
It never occurred to me until I heard you say those
things out loud that no, in fact, one does *not* "gotta be
me" at all costs. On the contrary, the "me" is a matter of choice. It is empowering to change the "me" to
honor commitments, not, as I'd always assumed, the
other way around. I paid an excruciatingly high price
being "me" at the expense of my commitments. Your
seminar was like an elevator ride up from hell.

If you tell yourself you have one personality, you limit your
range of action. When you label yourself as "shy" or "lazy" or
"cowardly" or "disorganized," you shut down your ability to
make a magnificent gesture. You rule out being great. You
weave a cocoon for yourself to live inside. You might pray for
some circumstance to break you free, but the problem is that
you simply don't understand where the power is.

The power is not *out there*. It is in you.

5

We Make Ourselves Miserable or Strong

OWNERS SEE PROBLEMS AS BODYBUILDERS see weight: more resistance to build a life with. It's resistance training, and it feels good.

Victims, on the other hand, don't want to lift that weight. They look at weights with horror, and they look at problems as betrayals.

The sad tragedy is that the *same energy* that could be going into problem-solving is used by the victim for problem-avoidance. It takes an ongoing mental effort to push problems out of the mind. It is real work to constantly redirect the spotlight of consciousness away from life so that it shines only on distractions.

"We either make ourselves miserable," said the Brazilian sage Carlos Castaneda, "or we make ourselves strong. The amount of work is the same."

It's almost as if the victim's miserable life's work is to avoid things. And by avoiding things, victims create even more misery than they avoid. It's not the problems themselves that make them miserable (as they think), it's their own deliberate act of avoidance that lowers their self-esteem and ruins their self-respect.

The first thing victims think must be avoided is embarrassment. "What would people think?" is the automatic question that pops into their minds before considering any action.

The habit of avoiding embarrassment—and the accompanying chronic worry about other people's judgments—usually begins in junior high school and then never leaves. That's when the neural pathways are dug, and later deepened, which means that most people form their permanent identities in junior high school.

But have we done this intentionally? Of course not! Who would knowingly choose a life designed by a teenager? But that's exactly what we've done. We've tried to live lives designed by teenagers! No wonder they are nightmares!

The first step on the way out is to see how we got there. We need to find the relaxation to know "who we are" and just how ethereal that mask really is.

People who feel stuck inside a personality don't realize that they have a strong spirit self deeper inside. They are so hypnotized by "who they are" that they don't know who they can be.

When he was a frustrated young man at the end of his teenage years, British author Colin Wilson was so depressed he decided to kill himself. He obtained a bottle of cyanide, and was ready to do the act. Just as he was about to drink the poison, he heard a voice. It was a completely different voice than his own personality's voice. It came from deep inside him, and it shouted, *What are you doing??!!* and he put down the bottle of poison. His suicidal thoughts were over, forever. His everyday self gave way to that hidden, stronger self at the last minute. Today, Wilson recalls the event with humor: "I realized that if Colin Wilson killed himself," he said, "I'd be dead too! And that wouldn't do."

Something short of Nirvana

Many people never hear that stronger voice inside them. A voice as big as the universe. They have habitually given all their power to the weary everyday voice that is reactive to everyone and everything. They think that everyday self is all there is.

This handwritten note was found on a telephone message board next to the body of a commodities broker. He had just shot himself:

Somebody had to do it. Self-awareness is everything.

It was obviously too late to wake him up and tell him that he had gotten it all wrong, that the "self" he was too painfully aware of was only the shallow and fatigued everyday made-up self. There were more selves up the ladder of consciousness. He had selves inside who could have helped him see the beauty of life, but he had fallen into the habit of ignoring them, so they lost their light and power.

In his study of suicide notes titled . . . *Or Not to Be,* Marc Etkind contrasts the self-victimizing thinking of the late Kurt Cobain with the ownership spirit of his wife, Courtney Love.

Cobain was the lead singer of the grunge rock group Nirvana. His addiction to heroin was a major factor in the death he chose: a shotgun blast to the head that was so powerful, police had to use fingerprints to identify the body.

He had written a long, poetically self-pitying suicide note to his family and fans that his wife, performer Courtney Love, used to read at her own concerts.

While publicly reading Cobain's suicide note, Courtney Love interspersed his words with her own. She became strong as she read the note, refusing to be the second victim of the tragedy. She showed her anger and her *spirit* when she asked why he didn't simply quit music if he was so tired of it?

She referred to his letter mockingly as a "letter to the editor," and ended the reading by yelling out to the crowd, "Just tell him he's a [jerk], okay? . . . and that you love him."

Curt had contracted down into that smallest known, and most painful element in the universe: "me."

6

The Ultimate Mass Seduction

I RECENTLY RECEIVED A LARGE glossy envelope in the mail from one of the nation's more famous self-help authors and speakers. It promised that you could "change your body as effortlessly as you change your clothes."

This was the same speaker who at another time said that you didn't really have to *read* his books (because we all know how hard reading is), but you could just "metabolize" them by looking at the words in them for a few moments each day.

Our country has evolved from having an enthusiastic work ethic (brought here by immigrants eager to build and grow) into a comfort-obsessed, passive mass audience searching for a hassle-free existence.

This aversion to effort can also be found in the demonization of the concept of willpower. Almost every new transformational program promises up front that "this has nothing to do with willpower!" Thank God! Then I'm willing to listen. And then I'm willing to buy.

"Willpower doesn't work!" the victim cries. But how would he know? He's never experimented with it.

Driving down the road yesterday, I heard a radio ad for a new system for learning a foreign language. The radio personality endorsing the new "cyber" system of language learning said the great thing about it was that you didn't have to do any real work. "I learned Spanish myself with almost no effort at all!" he crowed. "All you do is put on the headphones and *listen!*"

I noticed that he didn't show off his Spanish to us. I also noticed that his voice, while pretending to be enthusiastic, was the voice we all associate with insincerity. He was reading copy. It thought it might be fun to drop him into a Mexican jungle full of cartel members to see how his new language would work.

What if everyone in America did everything they could to avoid effort—and yet the secret of happiness was, in fact, the effort?

I'll make a subliminal effort only

I have to confess that the first 35 years of my own life were spent looking for the easier, softer way. And as I described more extensively in my book on self-motivation *(100 Ways to Motivate Yourself)*, I came to a jarring but liberating realization along the easier, softer way: The easier I am on myself, the harder life is on me.

I entered the U.S. Army after a few years in college because I thought I needed some self-discipline. Can you see the mistake in that? I couldn't.

I had not really examined the phrase *self*-discipline. My mind had automatically cancelled out the "self" part. So I thought someone else could self-discipline me!

I have bought many books over the years with which to improve myself. Before I realized what true self-motivation was, I would always look for the tape or book that made self-improvement look effortless. A typical title on my shelves is *Grow Rich While You Sleep*. The author who wrote that book sure knew his audience. I snatched that one up without even opening it.

I bought subliminal tapes because they required the least effort of all. You don't even have to actively listen to them! Just play them somewhere near you. Perfect.

Someone come make me strong. Please hurry.

I was attracted to self-help programs that featured affirmations and visualization because they are sold mainly for their *effortless* nature. With affirmations, you just repeat words over and over. You don't have to believe the words to say them. *And you don't have to do anything.* You just wander around muttering things, like the Dick Tracy character, Mumbles. Transformation is achieved effortlessly.

Then I got absorbed by books and courses that taught visualization as the key to success. All you do is put on some soothing music and close your eyes and picture things. That's it. Dream about your future. It's out there, beyond the second star.

"But don't I have to do anything?" I once asked a facilitator of a visualization workshop.

"No," he said. "Just close your eyes. Your future will come to you."

"I don't have to make an effort?" I asked.

"No!" he said. "This isn't about willpower. This is about faith. Faith is the most beautiful thing on earth. All you need is faith and belief and you have it all. If you close your eyes and believe it with all your heart, you will have it."

This sounded ideal to me. Faith, hope, and wishful thinking were just what I knew I could be good at. I started thinking back to Peter Pan and Wendy, and how wonderful it would be to simply stand in my parents' window and shout, "I won't grow up!" and then if they asked me to make any effort at all, I would just fly away.

Don't work smarter, work harder

Later, as I became more and more involved in businesses, I became attracted to books and programs that recommended, "Don't work harder; work *smarter!*" I liked that, because some of my goals were beginning to look like they might involve some real effort, and I was worried about my capacity to pull that off.

The biggest *lie* humankind has told itself over the past 50 years is that success is available without effort; that effort is unnecessarily painful; that effort is not valuable, and, indeed, is to be avoided whenever possible. It is a retirement of ease and comfort is something "you owe yourself" and that only a thoughtless fool exerts any real energy in the course of a given day.

It is a lie that enters the human biocomputer like a virus. Then the virus gets transferred from one biocomputer to another like this:

"Hey, you ought to get some of those pills! I lost 15 pounds in two weeks. I didn't have to *do anything!*"

Perhaps the "effortless" virus in my biocomputer might tell yours that you ought to join this religious cult. It's great. The heavenly guru does all your thinking for you. You just have to passively follow. It's effortless. Tomorrow we're drinking Kool-Aid and putting plastic bags over our heads so we can join the big spaceship. Come on along. It's really easy! You don't have to *do anything.* They even tie the bags on *for you.*

I remember as a little boy finding out about heaven from my mother. I was 4 years old. I was standing beneath her ironing board as she ironed clothes.

"Do you have to do anything in heaven?" I asked her. "Any chores or anything?"

"No," she said. "That's the whole point of heaven. The lion lies down with the lamb."

"They don't fight? They don't kill each other?"

"No," said my mother. "It's as if they're on tranquilizers. Good ones. It's beautiful. Everything is soft and white. There are clouds, like dry ice everywhere. Nobody does anything. You, especially, are going to like it there."

The biggest intellectual breakthrough in the life of the great poet William Butler Yeats came when he realized that happiness and growth were the same thing. "Happiness is neither this nor that," he said. "Happiness is growth. We are happy when we are growing." You can notice this for yourself: You are happy when you are growing, are you not? And no growth you've ever made has ever been effortless.

Watch the nature film of a butterfly struggling to push through the cocoon. You will see effort. You will be moved by the effort. You will see the animating force within a living being. It's the force of a powerful reinvention. Watch the movie *Rocky*. You will see the hidden connection between effort and joy. Pay attention to your reactions to certain scenes in movies. Pay attention to your goose bumps and your tears. They come in response to courage and effort. They don't come in response to a scene in which someone is being comfortable. Pay attention to why you are choked up. It is your potential self trying to tell you something. It's the butterfly in your own cocoon. It wants out.

7

It's Not About Your Flesh and Blood

I AM NOT A SLICK salesperson. But I'm extremely successful "selling" my Owner–Victim seminars. I think it's because my enthusiasm for the subject immediately transfers to people listening to me.

But sometimes people—managers and CEOs trying to make a training decision—just don't get what this ownership spirit is. They think it must be some kind of mystical New Age "soft" training that will cause their people to get in touch with their inner Gandhis and dance barefoot from the room, never to be competitive again.

I like to give those CEOs a good strong competitive American metaphor they can relate to.

"Have you ever had a child play sports?" I ask them.

They almost always say yes.

"Then imagine that feeling you have when you watch your kid play. Let's say you have a daughter who plays on the softball team. There's that feeling you have when you're at the game, cheering for her, yelling for her team. It doesn't matter how tired you were before you got to the game. That feeling wipes it out. That feeling is the ownership spirit, and you created it inside of yourself on behalf of your daughter. My course teaches you how to create that spirit on behalf of your own life."

"Well, now, wait a minute," the CEO says. "Hold on. When I cheer for my daughter playing softball, it's because she's my kid. That feeling I get is a feeling *any father would get* in that situation. It just comes to you."

"No, it's not," I say. "That feeling is one you created. That's the ownership spirit created by you. That energy you bring to being a vocal fan of your daughter's team is self-generated. All team spirit is."

"I don't believe that," he says. "I think it comes to you naturally when you have your own kids out there. Watching your own flesh and blood play."

"It's not about flesh and blood," I say. "It's about the connection we all have to our spirit."

"I disagree," he says.

"Well then, let me ask you something. What if the daughter you have been cheering for all these years isn't really your daughter after all? Perhaps your wife had a better sense of humor than you realize. She just forgot to tell you. Yet you've been cheering for that kid, someone else's kid, all these years! Where did all *that* cheerful spirit come from?"

By now the CEO has become uncomfortable, but a little more open to the idea. What I want him to see is that whatever spirit we have inside—school spirit, team spirit, pure spirit—can be accessed through intentional creation. We're in charge of it.

"Do you have a dog?" I ask him.

"Yes," says the CEO. "He's just a little runt, but our family loves him."

"Well, good," I continue. "What if your little dog went across the street and you saw the neighbors throwing stones at him?"

"Those neighbors would regret that."

"Okay. So you have a pretty strong feeling of ownership for that little dog of yours. Where did *that* come from? That's not genetic, I hope. That's not flesh and blood."

He was beginning to see.

I asked a friend of mine recently what ownership means to him, and I got a really quick answer.

Fred Knipe is a four-time Emmy-award winning TV writer, actor, songwriter, and comedian who spreads the joy of human-identity folly through his writing and humor. The most creative work he's done, though, has been the work on his own life's direction. Whereas most people settle for a safe career inside something predictable, Fred has always followed his spirit into ever-widening circles of unconventional writing and performing. Each year that goes by, he increases his ownership of his career's path.

"To own something," he said, "means to declare that it belongs to you. To claim it. To make it a part of what you value and will defend. It can be a marriage, a friendship, a skill, a venture, a success, a mistake. We can own our values by declaring them. We can own our lives instead of pretending they belong to fate."

When you start to see the power in mentally owning things—in taking full creative possession of them—you'll own more and more situations and things. You won't want to pretend your life belongs to fate. Many of the external circumstances in your life seem to belong to fate, but so what? You won't be able to think of a circumstance you can't enjoy once you've decided to wrap your own spirit around it.

Once you own your own energy and spirit, you'll see the positive side of taking responsibility. Responsibility has gotten a bad name. We associate it with guilt and blame. But responsibility is magnificent if it's thought about with a high level of consciousness. Responsibility is powerful when thought of in its positive sense. It is the *ability* to choose our *responses*. It's our response skill; our "response ability."

When you learn to take full responsibility for setting a goal, you'll reach it in no time. When you learn to totally own a problem, the problem doesn't stand a chance. But because we're so afraid of the negative side of responsibility, we miss out on the sheer joy of cultivating *rapid response time.*

The thrill of a rapid response

Absolute focus is the key to all great human achievement. Its opposite, preoccupation, is the enemy of all achievement. Write this thought down, because it can change your life: *Preoccupation is the enemy of all achievement.*

In any activity, preoccupation is the enemy. It's true with cooking, love-making, driving, golf, gardening, painting, anything.

Taking ownership is the highest form of focus: It's a willingness to bring everything you've got to the situation. To live in the now. When you do that, your spirit wakes up to join you in the fun.

Too many strangers in the night

A woman told me the other day that she was feeling awful because she spent her Sunday afternoon and evening playing cards with her girlfriends when she really would have liked to have been with her daughter.

"Why didn't you tell your girlfriends *no*?" I asked.

"I didn't want to hurt their feelings. They asked me last week, too, and I couldn't do it then because my aunt was sick and I had to go stay with her."

"Did you want to play cards last weekend?"

"Yes, I did, because my daughter was out of town."

"Why didn't you?"

"Because my aunt was sick, and no one could stay with her."

"Why was that?"

"Her husband had a golf trip and he wasn't going to return until the next day."

"Why didn't you just say no?"

"I didn't want to hurt her feelings."

"So you are willing to sacrifice your relationship with your daughter so you won't have to say no?"

"I was taught never to hurt anyone's feelings. The other day a phone solicitor called during dinner and I left the table and talked to him for half an hour because I just couldn't hang up on him. But afterward I felt bad because my family ate without me. There I was talking to some stranger."

"Is the telephone solicitor more important to you than your family?"

"Of course not."

"Then why didn't you just tell him that and return to the table?"

"I couldn't be rude. I couldn't just hang up on him. I would never hang up on anybody. That's not how I was raised."

"You hung up on your family! You hang up on the people who are important to you all the time. Try to see that. Try to start saying no. All day long. No, no, no, no, no! Get your life back!"

I was a garden hose

My own life was directionless and in financial chaos for many years. My essential problem was lack of ownership. I was pathologically preoccupied. I had a thousand things going on at once. I had so little discipline and direction (the same thing, really) that I sprayed my thoughts everywhere. My consciousness was like a garden hose with the nozzle turned to mist: no focus, no power.

I thought of a thousand different things a day. My emotions were in control. Whenever a feeling came up, that's where my thinking went! I was the most distractible person on the planet. I was spread so thin, you could see right through me.

By thinking of a thousand different things every day, my life was ruined. I was like a millionaire who had deposited one single dollar into a million different banks. Living that way is a form of being so undisciplined that *anything* can pull your attention away. You can't say no to anything.

I hear many complaints from people I coach and work with who are going through the same kind of scattered lives. It's as if they're dying from a thousand tiny distractions, bleeding from a thousand little cuts. They report a life of being constantly drained by other people's requests, a life in which they have not learned to say no.

Your ability to invent who you want to be will depend on your willingness to develop a little-used muscle known as the "No Muscle." If you never use this muscle, it won't perform for you when the chips are down. It will be too weak to work. Any request by any coworker or relative will pull you from your life.

First, you flex the "Yes Muscle"

The key to developing the "No Muscle" is to first develop your "Yes Muscle." If you will first say yes to the things that are important to you, then saying no to what's not important will get easier and easier.

Your list of goals and priorities is a form of saying yes to what's important to you. When you cultivate the habit of setting aside specific time to do the things you love and to be with the people you love, it becomes very easy to say no to those who try to cut in on you. Life is a dance. Don't skip the dance.

If you plan a week in advance to take your son to lunch and a movie on Saturday, it's no problem at all saying no to someone who asks you to come help them move their furniture. "I've made a commitment to my little boy that I can't break," you say, and people understand.

The insanity starts when no goals, plans, or commitments are ever made and people you don't even care about are taking all your time. You can't say no to them only because you haven't said yes to anything else.

The greatest value of planning is that it gives you your own life to live. It allows you to continuously reinvent yourself toward strength and focus. It puts you back in charge. It allows you to focus on what's most important to you. So you won't walk around all the time singing the Broadway song, "I'm Just a Girl Who Can't Say No."

Ask yourself these questions: What goals are most important to me? How much time do I give them? What people are most important to me? How much time do I give them?

We become what we give our thoughts to. Reinvention begins with a plan to reinvent. The planning itself is your most important priority. Block out time each day for thinking and planning. It feels weird at first. Like you're not "doing anything." But you are. You will start to reap benefits beyond what you can anticipate. The planning time is so open and creative, you can't imagine ahead of time what you will discover. That's why most people don't do it. Fear of the unknown. But soon you'll discover that the unknown is on your side. It won't work against you. It is where everything good develops and blossoms.

8

Dying Inside Your Comfort Zone

THE COMFORT ZONE IS A place to rest, not to live.

Doug Grant fell from a scaffold on which he was working and wound up in the hospital temporarily paralyzed from the waist down.

After being in the hospital for a few days, he began to receive visits from nurses and counselors who were trying to help him deal with his situation. Trying to help him cope, psychologically.

"I was getting more and more upset with these people," he told me during a break at one of my seminars. "They kept asking me to learn to *deal with* being paralyzed. That was the last thing I wanted. I knew I needed my mind completely focused on what I wanted—to walk again."

Doug was convinced that if he focused on what he wanted instead of what he didn't want, he would find a way to get what he wanted.

"I finally had to tell them that the next person they sent in to tell me to 'deal with' my paralysis would have an opportunity to deal with their own."

Doug Grant not only got up and walked again, but he also won a gold medal in the world championships of weightlifting.

"After my accident," he said, "I made health and fitness my passion and my obsession."

He had taken over his "tragic" situation. He reinvented himself as an owner. Owners let everything and everyone become their teacher.

You fall, you learn.

Doug Grant was in a seminar of mine again recently, and during a break he came up to remind me of this story, because I had done such an incomplete job of answering one of the seminar attendee's questions. A young man had asked me the difference between an owner's and a victim's thinking when it came to the suffering of genuine pain. Doug Grant knew something about pain.

"If you focus on the pain, and think of nothing but the pain, you will not get anywhere," Doug pointed out. "You have to accept the pain for what it is, and then focus completely on what you want. The more you focus on what you want, the less the pain matters."

Owners focus on what they want. Victims focus on what they fear. And both positions are pure internal invention.

In the days after his accident, the nurses and counselors attempted to ease Doug Grant into a comfort zone. We assume, in our society, that comfort is always the ultimate good. We hear phrases during conversations and negotiations such as, "I just want something that we can both be comfortable with," and both people will take it as an unquestionable given that "comfort" is an ultimate value. But is it?

Even an ameoba prefers a challenge

People look forward to retirement because they imagine great comfort. What they often get is an increase in visits to the doctor, an increase in prescriptions, sometimes an increase in depression, and often an early death. The human system does not really want comfort, it wants challenge. It wants adventure.

And perhaps we can extend that from "the human system" to *all living beings*.

Stewart Emery reports a startling experiment done with amoebas in California. In his book *Actualizations,* he reveals how two tanks of amoebas were set up in order to study the conditions most conducive to growing living organisms.

In one tank, the amoebas were given ultimate comfort. The temperature, humidity, water levels, and other conditions were constantly adjusted for ultimate ease in living and proliferation. In the other tank, the amoebas were subjected to rude shocks. They were given rapidly whipsawing changes in fluid level, temperature levels, protein, and every other condition they could think of.

To the total amazement of the researchers, the amoebas in the more difficult conditions grew faster and stronger than those in the comfort zone. They concluded that having things too set and too perfect can cause living things to decay and die, whereas adversity and challenge lead to strength and the building of the life force.

This might also explain why suicide rates in America have always gone down during times of war. And why in Denmark, where a very comfortable government-run lifestyle is guaranteed to everyone, the suicide rate is the highest in the world. There is not much difference between death and the comfort zone. Crossing the line is easy.

The only difference between a rut and a grave is a few feet.

9

A Deadly Bait and Switch Game

When I was a boy, my father was my idol.

He was one of the most successful young businessmen of his generation. A war hero in World War II, he came home to embark on a career in business and lived his life at an enormously high level of energy.

It wasn't long before he was president and CEO of a number of industrial companies throughout the Midwest. He became the right-hand business partner of Warren Avis, of Avis Rent A Car.

When I was young, I remember flying with him in his small private plane to one or another of his companies in Pennsylvania and New York, and thinking that this man is the ultimate American hero.

When my father wasn't flying around the country building his businesses, he would often walk across the street to join me and my friends in a pick-up basketball game, which he would almost always win. He played like he owned the game.

"Desire," he used to say to me. "Desire is everything. If you have enough of it, you can do anything you want. I guarantee you. Anything."

My father used to take me to watch the Detroit Lions play football and he would point out the power of desire on the football field. His favorite football player was Doak Walker. Walker was a running back, but when the Lions got in a difficult and crucial defensive situation where they absolutely had to make a stop, they would put Doak Walker in. He was small, but his passion for defense made up for it. Walker was a fearless tackler who always seemed to know where the play was going.

My father loved showing me Doak Walker, and I knew that I was watching a player play the way my father was living his life. He was playing with desire.

Then something happened to my father's life.

Who knows how these things happen? Could it have to do with the 2,000 advertisements every American sees and hears each day about the desirability of comfort? Could it be so deep in our culture that we are certain that we "deserve a break today"?

I am now convinced that the voice that whispers, "Live a life of comfort," is the voice of evil. I can remember the seductive voice of Madonna in one of her songs whisper-singing, "Let's get unconscious, baby." It is painfully true that owners of the human spirit can sometimes be seduced. Owners can lose it completely. Look at Elvis. Look at Marlon Brando. Total owners early in life, and then victims of gluttony and comfort, ballooned up into the size of Thanksgiving Day parade floats, grotesque opposites of what they used to be. Owner to victim in nothing flat.

My father retired early. He was a multimillionaire in his 40s when he decided to kick back and take it easy and enjoy life. And drink himself to death.

His only real pleasure in his final 20 years of "comfortable" living was to remember the past. His stories would revisit the glory days of hardship and adventure. When he told me stories about his life, it was always about the things that had challenged him the most.

I loved my father dearly, and I still do when I think of him. Watching him die of comfort was similar to watching my other boyhood idol, Elvis Presley, do the same thing. I don't blame either of them. I honor them, and I promise myself I will not follow them. (Actually, I already *tried* following them and it nearly killed *me*.) In their own way, they have shown us the path to the zone, and we can use their lives as huge lessons. Or not.

My own attempts to drown in comfort early in my life taught me something I was lucky to live long enough to learn: Alcohol and drugs first feel as if they offer more life—an *effortless* route to the spirit. They seem at first to expand a dreary consciousness into something wilder and more free. But it is a chemical falsehood from the start. It's a major lie.

Addiction is a deadly bait and switch game, because soon the addict must use the substance just to feel like he did before he became addicted. He now needs the substance just to feel normal. Just to feel like he's having the average bad day of someone not addicted, the addict must score big and use heavily just to feel average! And it had seemed like such a great shortcut to the spirit.

All it proves is that chemicals produce a false spirit. This is not the true spirit. And because it is false, it turns on us. It behaves like anything we ever tried to *get quick* without effort.

Get rich quick. Get high. Get lucky.

Some universal vital principle always wants us to see that the effort itself is important—even beautiful. That effort in itself is good fortune. And to chemically try to avoid it will backfire in the grimmest way.

Notice for yourself what people are talking about when their eyes are glowing with happiness. It is almost always adversity or some challenge overcome, someone's first marathon, someone's first talk in front of his or her company, someone's big football game, a difficult childbirth. It's always something that took effort and courage. It's interesting to keep track of what excites people.

Notice, too, that no one talks much about comfort. If I were to write a book called *Great Moments in Human Comfort,* I don't think anyone would buy it unless he or she thought it was comical, which it surely would be.

On your death bed, you will not wish you had been more comfortable, or that you had found an even easier, softer pleasure zone to hide out in. You will wish you had ventured out more. That you had spoken up more. Tried some things. Reinvented yourself one more time.

10

Walk That Road
From Fear to Action

VICTIMS ARE FOND OF SAYING that we have no heroes today. But if they would step back, they would see the bigger picture: Potentially, we have *nothing but* heroes.

Every person is offered a hero's journey to take, and more than ever before in the history of the world, people are becoming aware of their individual journeys. More than ever before, people are taking responsibility for their own wisdom and adventure. Consider the remarkable continued popularity of the movie *The Wizard of Oz*.

Frank L. Baum's *Oz* books, which I devoured as a child, continue to appeal to people because they are a metaphor for the journey we all try to take. The journey is from absolute dependence on other people (begun in the womb) to a thrilling independence of others, characterized by a growing union with the spirit inside.

Why do so many families still rent *The Wizard of Oz* video when there are so many other exciting movies available?

We're off to see the wizard

The journey down the Yellow Brick Road is representative of everyone's journey in life. Most of us spend a lot of years looking for wizards who will *give us* the wisdom we need, the courage we need, and the heart we need to go on. In the movie, the wizard tells Dorothy and her friends that they had it all along. It was inside of them. The wizard didn't give anything to the Tin Man that he didn't already have.

Our own individual journey begins in the womb, where we are totally dependent. Our first surge of independence comes when we separate from our mother's body and become literally and physically independent of her.

The second surge on the journey is when we leave home and go out into the world to make a living for ourselves. For many people, this part of the journey to independence is so terrifying that they try to go back. For some, "going back" takes the form of finding a mate on whom to be totally emotionally dependent; someone who serves as a substitute parent. This never really works, because no mortal can provide such a service.

But if we could see clearly that we don't really need that kind of dependence, and that there are more and more stages and surges ahead on the journey to independence, we would keep going. We would keep on the journey, reinventing ourselves for the pure evolutionary joy of it all the way.

The knowledge of how to swim or ride a bicycle cannot be passed along, or taught in a seminar; it must be discovered in a deeply personal way by the individual. The same is true for the wisdom of staying on the journey.

I found a new place to dwell

Sometimes we make an astonishing early surge on the journey to independence and don't even realize what we have done. If you look at the life of Elvis Presley, you see in his first TV appearances a joyful independence and courage that fascinated the entire world. No white person had ever sung with so much energy and passion. No white person had ever set the spirit free on stage with so much abandon. (Al Jolson had tried, but he felt he had to dress up as an African-American person to get away with it.)

Prior to Elvis, white people singing on stage looked like Clutch Cargo cartoons, with only their mouths moving in an otherwise-passive body. Their cautious voices would not melt an icy heart.

I remember when I was 13 years old, sitting in front of my TV at home in suburbanly tranquilized Birmingham, Michigan, watching Elvis Presley on the Tommy Dorsey and Ed Sullivan shows, and how I was stunned. Could you really feel that and sing like that with so much freedom and raw joy? How could anyone dare to sing with that kind of range and power while smiling like the canary who ate the cat? Life became full of new possibilities I'd never dreamed of. Who was it possible to be?

I had never seen a self invented quite like that, such an owner of the spirit. Elvis owned the songs and he owned the crowd. His voice was slurred with surly joy as it soared through the ozone. He had blown a hole in the universe. (The word "universe" literally means "one song," and for me, Elvis was singing it.)

But the spirit soon began to fade for Elvis, because he didn't fully understand what he had. Like so many other stars, he sought shortcuts to continue the journey, and they were chemical.

Drugs and alcohol masquerade as courage and spirit, and users believe that the drugs keep the journey to independence going, because that's the temporary illusion they give.

But drugs and alcohol turn on the user and actually reverse the journey. They mimic and mock the human spirit: They are like Elvis impersonators. They impersonate the spirit. They give us false courage and "spirits" for a while, but soon they create a new deadly dependence—and this kind of dependence is exactly what we thought we were journeying away from. It was an illusion. For some, it's fatal.

Elvis began his life in the spirit. He broke out of the gate gloriously. People thought he had a weird personality because he had no personality. There was no fabricated person between him and the music. It was just the music singing through his human form. His early songs are still unmatched in raw energy and vocal range. But once he came home from the army, his dear mother dead and his inner spirit gone dim, he made the unconscious decision to journey backward. It was not a pretty sight. Those of us who had been inspired by him were now embarrassed to see his lazy, phony movies, and hear his voice thicken and contract with the abuse of drugs and deep-fried peanut butter and banana sandwiches.

Where have all the heroes gone?

Elvis was an early hero in my life because he showed me a vision of raw independence. He modeled the *spirit* for a generation of sit-at-home, repressed *Ozzie & Harriet* viewers stagnating in the suburbs during the Eisenhower years. (Even Little Ricky had been inspired by Elvis to reinvent himself.)

Victims claim we no longer have heroes, but that's not true. If we would open our eyes, we would see more heroes than ever before. The first one each day is right there in the mirror.

Victims long for the old heroes such as Babe Ruth and JFK, but they were no greater heroes than the heroes of today; they just benefited from being fictionalized by the media, which looked the other way when they drank heavily or chased women. To say Babe Ruth is my hero is like saying that Santa Claus is my hero.

One person I have always enjoyed being inspired by is the late actress Jessica Tandy. She never quit the journey. Even in her 80s, she kept growing in her independence and blossoming spirit. Unlike most people who use the aging process as a self-pitying excuse to avoid effort, she was always becoming new to herself. Always reinventing.

Even in her final screen performances, in *Driving Miss Daisy* and *Nobody's Fool,* she showed the world how amazing we human beings can be. To Jessica Tandy, the journey was never over. And you could see that commitment in her work. If you watch *Driving Miss Daisy* or *Nobody's Fool,* you can answer for yourself the question of whether you ever have to grow old.

Keep track of your own spiritual journey. Be aware of it; think of it often. Have it be big to you. Have it be beautiful. It's not there to scare you; it's there to excite you.

Know which direction on the journey you're going at all times. Is this decision you're about to make taking you toward or away from independence? (The paradox is that you become more emotionally independent as you become more aware of your spiritual connection to all living things.) Which is the road you really want to take? The road back to dependency and infantilism is the road more traveled, but you won't want to take it when you see where it leads.

By being conscious of your journey, you can drop all the old excuses. You can stop using "growing older" as a reason to lessen your effort and activities. You can step things up. You can effect a quickening. You can take over the controls of your own energy system. Why not? You did it as a child. Just do it again, this time with consciousness and wisdom. You'll see your new life in your energy, and you'll finally see that reinvention is there for the sheer fun of it.

11

The Rapid Beauty of Enthusiasm

FOR A LONG WHILE IN our society, enthusiasm was embarrassing. We tried to hide it. "Cool" was in; enthusiasm wasn't.

Here's an example. Originally, Jay Leno wanted to write his life story as it actually happened. He wanted to tell how enthusiastic he was about becoming a big-time comedian and star, and how much drive and purpose his life took on. He wanted to tell the world that anyone could have done his or her own version of it, and he wanted to link his success to hard, obsessive, concentrated, purposeful work.

So excited was Jay Leno about the power of the formula he had found for success that he wanted to call his autobiography, *A Good Dog Will Run Till its Heart Explodes*.

But slicker minds prevailed and the culture of the day won out. There was too much raw enthusiasm in the title *A Good Dog Will Run Till its Heart Explodes*. So they talked him into calling his book *Leading With My Chin*. Jay had an odd looking, very large chin, and it was "cooler" in this day and age to make fun of a physical defect than to praise a passion for succeeding and becoming great.

So Jay didn't get to tell us the real uncool secret of his success: that something magical happens when one is willing to *go for it*. Instead, he presented a self-conscious, vulgar, self-deprecating autobiography full of cutesy stories that made him look sleazy and self-effacing, for a laugh. It wasn't the *real* Jay Leno. He caved in to the shallow autobiography because purposeful, focused work was not politically correct. People think there can't be any reason for such a passion for good work other than greed and ego; therefore it is always better to play it down. You don't want to embarrass yourself.

Leno's success, though, has been a tribute to focus. We secretly love how he did it. We are starting to lose patience with the scattered, distracted life brought about by massive appeals to comfort and ease. We're tired of the electric toothbrush and the ubiquitous cell phone, and pop culture is beginning to reflect that: I saw a bumper sticker the other day that said, "Hang Up and Drive!"

I believe that people are also tired of this political correctness that says hard work is greedy and enthusiasm for one's career is just ego. I believe we secretly long for enthusiasm. That's why enthusiasm is in the process of making a huge comeback.

People went to watch movies such as *Jerry Maguire* because when the actor Cuba Gooding, Jr., jumped around yelling, "Show me the money! Show me the money!" he was demonstrating raw enthusiasm, and we secretly loved it. The reason that phrase became so annoyingly popular was because someone was showing unembarrassed enthusiasm for something we are usually "cool" about: money.

In the Julia Roberts movie *My Best Friend's Wedding,* an entire table of people together begins singing "I Say a Little Prayer for You" with such enthusiasm that the whole audience was overwhelmed. Some of us in the theater had tears in our eyes.

In Tom Hanks's exuberant masterpiece *That Thing You Do,* the transcendent scene occurs when the kids in the rock band hear their song on the radio for the first time. Their unbridled excitement, running through the streets and stores, shouting and dancing for joy, makes the whole movie great.

Leonardo DiCaprio's character in *Titanic* was a human embodiment of the concept of enthusiasm. His love of life transcended danger and death itself. It transformed lives. It was the secret inside the movie *Titanic* that made the music beautiful and lifted the feelings of the entire world. We like seeing proof that the heart will go on.

Enthusiasm is our secret passion.

People listen to Dick Vitale, not because of what he knows about college basketball, but because of how enthusiastic he feels about it.

Now we're getting out of the house to go to movie theaters to see the thing we are missing most in our lives: enthusiasm. Tom Hanks in *The Terminal* inspires everyone with his innocent zest for life.

Notice that the most memorable and moving scenes in movies in recent years almost all involve people discarding their personalities and expressing pure spirit. We are paying good money to see that, because it's exactly what we know we want more of in our own lives.

It was this enthusiasm for life that Welsh poet Dylan Thomas was urging his dying father to find when he said, "Do not go gentle into that good night / but rage, rage against the dying of the light."

The word *enthusiasm* comes from the Greek *en theos,* which means "the God within." Getting connected to that part of us is the best experience we know.

Building the voice of "Yes!"

Your feelings of enthusiasm will always be the result of an internal effort you have made, whether you're aware of the effort or not. It is the result of something you've created through motion and movement, even if the movement is only in your spirit.

That "Yes!" feeling you get when you're enthused is a result of moving up to a higher level of imagination and spirit, and the knowledge that you moved yourself there. Like the butterfly pushing through the cocoon. Like Rocky running through the streets of Philadelphia in the early morning rain. That haunting musical theme to the movie *Rocky* became a part of our national history because it was about effort. *Rocky* was not about winning. Rocky didn't even win his fight. It was about something more inspiring than that.

Knowing the way to your spirit is three-fourths of the battle: seeing it, knowing it, realizing it, and staying awake to it.

In my own life, I had a lot of problems early on in getting out of my victim thinking and into my owner thinking, because I just didn't see how much I could do it. I thought I was trapped. The trap was tender, but it still felt like a trap. Inside the trap echoed the soft voice of the victim: "Well, what can you do? There's nothing you can do." But there was always a lot I could have done. I didn't see it, that's all.

To prove to yourself that there's always something you can do, try this experiment: Take out a clean, lined sheet of paper. On the top of your sheet of paper, list a problem you now have, some situation you wish were not there, some frustrating situation that you think about a lot but don't know what you can do about. I'm about to show you that your spirit knows.

Now, under the problem, write this sentence: "Five Small Things I Could Do About This Today." Then number 1 through 5 on the page with space beneath each one for your ideas. Don't get up until you've written the five things. Force yourself to write something.

Once you've written the five ideas, take the paper with you throughout the day and don't go to bed until all five things are done. Remember: These are little things you can do.

By the time you're finished, you will be surprised at how you have altered the nature of your problem. In many cases, you will have solved it completely. In other cases, you will see in your mind that it is no longer a problem, but, instead, a new *project*. A work in progress.

Do this a few times and you'll start to see what Thomas Jefferson meant when he said, "The more you do, the more you *can* do."

And why is that? It's because you have reinvented yourself from victim to owner. You had been a victim of the big, cloudy, unruly problem. And then you became the owner of a project that you yourself created. When you listed the five small things you could do, you turned it into your own intellectual property.

12

I Decided to Stop Being Weak

I REMEMBER ONCE, NOT VERY long ago, when my invented self was becoming unnecessarily weak. My coach could see it, but I couldn't.

My coach and mentor Steve Hardison had a tendency to go nonlinear on me when I deliberately pictured myself as weak and limited.

Many years ago, he had seen 10 percent of me that was most worth saving, and he showed me how to make that part all of me. He taught me reinvention.

No one I know of has had Hardison's track record in consulting, and no one I know of brings as much intelligent passion to the coaching as he does. Hardison finds the best in a person, and then treats the person as if he or she is *only* that best part. Soon, the best part grows. The rest falls away, dying of neglect.

In his home, Steve has framed and hanging in clear view a quotation from Nathaniel Branden:

I am convinced that one of the most helpful things we can do for people is to refuse to buy into their inappropriately restricted views of their limitations.

After my first successful two-year tour out on my own as a public speaker, I requested of Steve Hardison that he help me join one of the nation's foremost corporate training organizations. I felt the company would benefit from adding me to the staff of speakers and consultants, and that I'd benefit even more from working closely with their many Fortune 500 clients. But negotiations to join the company were going slowly.

Hardison was not pleased with the way I had approached the company, and believed that I felt a lot more strongly about how good I had become as a public speaker than I had let on. He thought I was being inappropriately restricted in my self-confidence and self-respect.

"Why can't you speak powerfully about who you really are?" he asked. "Why don't you let them know . . . really know . . . how powerful your presentations have become and how you really see yourself compared to other so-called motivators? If you're not committed to who you are, who else will be? Put it in writing. Be crisp about it, and be bold. Tell them who you are. Stop fooling around. The reason this job negotiation is going so slowly is *you*. *You* are responsible for the life you get, every bit of it."

So I went home to think about it. Why do I have to do this? Don't they already know? They already have my convention speaker's evaluations and testimonials. Do I have to *say* who I am?

And it was dawning on me that yes, I do have to say who I am. And by having the courage to say who I am, I will simultaneously create who I am. We "sentence" ourselves to the lives we get by who we say we are.

Take a walk on the wild side

So I went home and wrote a letter. I remembered something the great American sports journalist Red Smith said about how to write powerfully: You just open a vein and write. So I took a deep breath and I wrote a letter to the training company I wanted to work for.

"Here is what I am up to," I wrote. *"And what I will do* with or without *your company:*

"I will give the entire world *the most easy and entertaining access ever given to the principles of self-motivation and spiritual joy (infinite possibility) through drama and humor.*

"For example, my son Bobby's 4th-grade teacher had asked for copies of one of my books to pass around the school. His bus driver saw him with a copy of it and asked if she could read it. The bus driver read the book over spring vacation and then told Bobby she would be willing to pay for a large number of copies to give her friends and family. This struck me as important, because bus drivers do not usually read the literature of our profession.

"Here is what is missing *in our field of personal growth and achievement: simplicity and humor. We have secular evangelists teaching the principles instead of real, vulnerable people. The principles are being taught by squeaky clean boy scouts. These guys don't look or sound*

like they ever took a walk on the wild side or danced with the devil by the light of the moon.

"Bus drivers want this stuff, too, but they can't get into it if it's taught by people who look like morticians and sound like straight-A students who always brought an apple in for the teacher and dreamed of someday being *the teacher. We need to share this experience, not teach it.*

"Who I am for people is someone they can laugh with and identify with. I am the coward they've been waiting to hear from.

"And this exchange of experience I will do is through books that are not *intellectual justifications of my own authority. The problem with most of what we now see in personal-growth literature is that it was not written for the reader's sake. It was written as intellectual justification— proof that the writer is some kind of expert.*

"My books are for the bus drivers. They are especially for people who don't normally read. I know my books will someday set the country free, just as Napoleon Hill's books set us free in the 1950s.

"Being considered an expert is of no interest to me at all. In fact it works against my commitment to become one with my audience. I just want to testify."

I delivered the letter and got the job the next day.

Part Two

Owning
Relationships

Life is a comedy for those who think,
and a tragedy for those who feel.

—Horace Walpole

13

To Love Is to Play
the Numbers

TO AN OWNER OF THE spirit, love is not a dark, disturbing mystery. Love is like every other form of energy in the universe: The more you give, the more you get.

When my daughter Margie was 9 years old, she came to me one day with an upset look on her face.

"What's wrong, Margie?"

"Why does Stephanie get so many letters?" she asked in a sad little victim's voice. Stephanie, her older sister, was 11 at the time. "Stephanie gets letters all the time," she continued, "and I don't get any letters. It's not fair."

I knew just the question to gently ask Margie.

"Well, do you *write* any letters?"

"What do you mean?"

"Do you write any letters and send them out?"

"Well, no," she said, "because I don't know if I'll get any letters back. If I write letters and then don't get any back, it will be worse than it is now. I'll be even more disappointed.

Because how do you know? You don't know if you'll get a letter back."

"No," I said, "you don't know. You never know."

"Well, then, why do it?"

"Because you might."

"But what if I don't? That would be more sad."

"Yes, that would be sad."

"So I'm not going to do it."

"That's okay. You don't have to."

"But then how will I ever get letters?"

"You won't."

"I *know* that, because I don't get any letters now. And Stephanie gets a lot of letters."

"Because Stephanie writes a lot of letters."

"If I wrote a lot of letters, would I get letters back?"

"I'm pretty sure you would."

"But you don't know."

"No, I don't know. I can't promise you that you would."

Margie then gave me that look of frustration that tells me that she doesn't approve of how the universe is arranged. She went off to her room and I didn't give it another thought until a couple of days later when she came to me with an enormous pile of envelopes addressed in her handwriting. She asked, "Will you take these to your work today? Will you mail these for me?"

That was many years ago, and still today we are receiving letters in our mailbox to Margie, whose correspondences originated in that original windfall of writing. Margie, in that one instance, learned how love works. I hope she hangs on to the lesson all her life.

Notice that a victim rarely wants to do what Margie eventually did. Because a core belief of the victim is that life is unfair. Therefore, the victim never wants to risk anything. The victim never wants to go first in a relationship. "Why risk loving? I might get hurt!" The victim's feeling about love is an extended version of that one thought: "I'll write to them after they write to me."

The universe will pay it back

Writing letters represents any form of reaching out. You can create more peaceful relationships by "going first." The first step is to know who to go first with. Keep a list in your daily planner, or on an index card posted above the phone, of the most important people in your life.

Actually take the time to make this list. It sounds like an odd idea because our culture has convinced us that relationships are about spontaneous feelings, that we should always be responding to some inner spontaneous emotion, some internal organ bursting on its own. But great relationships are artfully *designed* like great homes and gardens.

Try creating that list of people who are important to you and keeping it nearby. Take it on vacations with you. Write those people postcards. When you have a free 20 minutes, pull the list out. Make a phone call. Add a name now and then.

Look at your list at least once a week and ask yourself whether you've communicated with these people lately. Communication can be short and clever and kind. It doesn't have to be a burden. Notes, cards, voice mails, e-mails, visiting, phone calls—they all count. Don't wait for the other people. Don't let your resentment undermine your creativity. Resentment goes away when *you* take action, not when the other person does. Don't ever wait. Resentment lives in a stagnant personality. Action eliminates it. Be action, don't be that person you were.

Consult your list at least once a day and get into action on at least one name. Help someone. Don't ever look at the list without taking action. Link the list to action. You'll be amazed at two things: 1) what comes back to you, and 2) how confident and serene you feel when you think of the people in your life. Guilt will leave you forever.

"If you help others, you will be helped," said the Russian spiritual teacher Gurdjieff. "Perhaps tomorrow, perhaps in a hundred years, but you will be helped. Nature must pay off the debt. It is a mathematical law and all life is mathematical."

The reinvention here is all about being in action. One reinvents from a passive, unappreciated person to the action of helping and communicating. Reinvention is always best when it takes you from noun to verb.

14

We Are Climbing Up the Ladder

THE WOMAN CONFRONTED ME IN a supermarket.

I was shopping and staring at some boxes of Cocoa Puffs on the shelf and she walked right up to me.

"Hey!" she said. "Don't I know you? Don't you teach that course on building relationships?"

I wasn't sure what was to follow, so I drew on a long history of cowardice and responded with equivocation.

"Well, I do teach some. . . ."

"No, I'm sure it's you. It was a year ago. I want to thank you."

"Oh, you liked the course?"

"Yes!"

"The relationship course? Yes, that was me."

"There was one part of that course that I have used ever since then."

"What was that?"

"The one thing, the best thing in your course was *the ladder*. There isn't a day goes by that I don't use that in my mind.

Sometimes during a conversation that isn't going well, I just picture it quickly, and I'm okay again. I want to thank you."

"The ladder. . . ," I said, not fully comprehending what she was talking about.

"Yes, you know, the ladder. And how we get stuck so low on the ladder we can't understand the other person we're talking to. . . ."

"Oh," I said. "The ladder. The ladder of selves?"

"The ladder of selves. Yes."

And it finally hit me what she was talking about. A year or so previously, during a question-and-answer session in one of the courses, I used British philosopher Colin Wilson's theory of the ladder of selves to answer someone's question.

"That was the best part of the course?" I asked the woman in the grocery store.

"By far," she said.

And so it came to my awareness that the best part of my course wasn't even in the course. It had been mentioned, almost accidentally, in one of the courses, but it wasn't a regular part of the course. That day in the store, I made a mental note to make certain "the ladder" was presented up front at the beginning of each course on building relationships.

Thinking leads to optimism

There's no question anymore in my mind that Colin Wilson is the most brilliant and profound philosopher since Aristotle. Since discovering him a few years ago, I have read more than 30 of his books, some of them three and four times. I can't help returning to them over and over again. His deep understanding of the human mind and his radiant optimism set him apart from all other writers and thinkers in the 20th century. So many of those writers are sophisticated victims.

One of Wilson's many illuminating concepts is "the ladder of selves," which illustrates how many different people we can all be. The lowest rungs on the ladder are the physical selves. They require the least amount of consciousness and mental wakefulness.

In the middle of the ladder are the emotional selves. These take a little more consciousness. When I'm in my emotional self, I am reacting to you. I am reacting with resentment, or fear, or guilt, or anger. If I travel up a few rungs, I reach some more positive emotions, such as peacefulness and mild euphoria, but they are still emotions without a great deal of consciousness or thinking.

Higher up the ladder is where great relationships are created. The higher rungs on the ladder are thoughtfulness, mindfulness, imagination; higher still: pure spirit.

We will almost always find that during the days of courtship, we are at the top of our ladders. During that period when we are most excited about falling in love with someone new is when it can be almost guaranteed that we are spending a huge percentage of time high up the ladder.

During courtship, we are using our minds. We are in our imaginations. We are creating all the time. Some of us write poetry, even though we don't normally write poetry. We are funny. We are clever. We are innovative and leave thoughtful little gifts around. We listen with more curiosity and compassion than ever before. We are in love, and we are seeing life from very high on our ladders. We are fascinated with the other person in a very light and joyful way. Every little breeze seems to whisper their name.

Because being high up the ladder is a thrill, most people will do almost anything to repeat the experience. The tragedy occurs when people confuse the *external stimulus* with their own power to ascend the rungs. They don't realize that they've *sent themselves* up. They think their new love sent them up. Or the exciting football game. Or getting a new job.

Because people so often associate being up the ladder with falling in love with someone fresh and new, they seek to repeat the experience outside their current relationship. This is unnecessary and is based on a misunderstanding of the ladder.

Your ladder of selves is internal. External excitements only remind you that it's there. The key to finding your spirit in life is to know that the ladder is on the inside, and that you can ascend it any time you want.

What keeps us down on the lower rungs is the paralyzing thought that we are simply who we are. That we will never change because, after all, once we have a personality, we are stuck with it. We create a story about who we are, and then add stories that confirm the first stories.

Reinventing yourself is not about replacing one story with another. It's about going up your ladder so high that there is no story to live up to. There is no permanent you. There is only action and rest. And the action is as exciting as life can be.

But when I sink back down into my heavily weighted story, the story of me, I slide down the ladder and I (hopefully) recall the words of Rudyard Kipling who wrote, "We are done with hope and honor / We are lost to love and truth / We are dropping down the ladder rung by rung."

15

The Ladder Lives Inside You

THE PAIN OF ALLOWING A relationship to lose its original thrill is usually unnecessary, but it is still painful nonetheless, and great songwriters have written about it for ages.

In Jim Webb's "Scissors Cut," Art Garfunkel sings:

"If they ever drop the bomb," you said,
"I'll find you in the flames."
And now we act like people
who don't know each other's names.

We assume that this loss of feelings is due to something external—the other person. Or we say, "The chemistry is just gone. Nothing I can do about *that!*" And so we try to chase it down again with a new lover. But it isn't long before we once again lose the feeling. It isn't long before you and I, once so in love, act like people who don't know each other's names.

Divorce rates go up and up as people confuse minor irritations and boredom with irreconcilable differences. (A man in Tariffville, Connecticut, filed for divorce after his wife left him a note on the refrigerator. Her note read, "I won't be home when you return from work. Have gone to the bridge club. There'll be a recipe for your dinner at 7 o'clock on Channel 2.")

And most of this filing for a change of partners is not necessary.

Ask Elizabeth Taylor.

Confusing and collapsing the thrill of being high up her ladder with the act of marrying someone, Elizabeth Taylor was married eight times in her life.

However, it appeared to me, as I watched her once in an interview with Barbara Walters, that she finally "got" what the woman in the grocery store "got" in my course. The ladder is inside, not outside. And she can send herself up or down regardless of who is in her life at the time.

"If you ever hear about me getting married again," she told Barbara Walters, "come slap me!"

She went on to describe how happy she now at the time of the interview, and how she had come to peace with how to create that happiness for herself. And it didn't depend on some man or some new thrilling courtship.

As Colin Wilson describes it, most of us spend our time "upside down" with our negative emotions on top and our imaginative thinking submerged and suffocated. Then some external crisis or adventure (such as falling in love) puts us "right side up" again. We credit the crisis, though, for doing something we did internally. This is the biggest mistake we humans make: confusing the outside with the inside.

Perhaps someone in our family has a problem with an addiction, and we all go through the recovery process together, attending "family week" at the treatment center, talking to each other like never before. We end up feeling "high." We *are* high! We are high up the ladder. We think the crisis did it. But it didn't; we did it.

What we don't understand is that, with practice and attention, we can learn to *put ourselves* right side up regardless of the external circumstance. Actually, right side up is where we belong. It's our natural state. You can see this in children. The happy thrill of being alive. Only our negative beliefs can bring us down the ladder. And as Byron Katie so convincingly explains in *Loving What Is*, none of those negative beliefs turn out to be true.

Happiness comes from playing

The ladder is like a piano in that mastering it takes practice. But once you've gotten some skill in ascending it, your life will become happier because you can make and keep relationship commitments with the absolute certainty that you need not fear or respond to your own emotions. You can put the "thrill" back into a marriage or friendship any time you want to make that effort. You can allow that excited, optimistic, new feeling back into your life at any time.

Inner peace and total relaxation is what will float you up the ladder. When you lose your connection to that inherent peace, your energy begins to leak and you will notice yourself sliding down the ladder. Don't ever feel bad about it, because at least you are now able to notice it, and *noticing* is 75 percent of the journey to enjoying your own life. Most people slide down their ladders many times a day and then stay down because they don't even know the ladder is there.

The existence of this internal, psychological, neurological ladder is a secret to most of our society and culture. Most of us still believe that someone or something can make us happy, that it all starts on the outside.

But that false belief is the very mistake that led Jean-Paul Sartre to say, "Hell is other people." Sartre was confusing the outside with his own inside.

This misunderstanding is just like the mistake of thinking the world was flat. People concluded that the world was flat because it seemed pretty obvious. Our senses looked at the outside world and reacted. Just as it seems pretty obvious that other people can make us happy or sad. But just because it seems obvious doesn't mean it's true.

The world is *not* flat. And thinking that it was flat kept people from venturing out. It kept people at home. Ancient couch potatoes were fearful of falling off the edge of the world if they went out too far.

Thinking that other people make us happy is the same kind of limiting superstition. It keeps us at home, on the couch, fearful of venturing out. Afraid that if we reach out for someone, we might fall off the edge of the world.

You can now see that this fear was a superstition based on a negative set of overwhelming feelings. You don't have to relate to people in that cautious, restricted way. *Your* world can become less flat and more round, too. (In fact, you can have a ball.)

16

You Can Climb a Stairway to Heaven

THE REALITY OF THE LADDER of selves can also be discovered by noticing our language. The way we speak to each other reveals its existence.

"Rise above it," we say. And most people can identify with what it feels like to rise above something that is bothering them.

Something bothers me only when I am down on the emotional rungs of my ladder. When I rise above it, I see the bigger picture. The bigger the picture I see, the smaller my troubles look. The more possibilities I see, the more the world is suddenly full of solutions. It always feels great to see the world from 10,000 feet.

And the more I rise above something, the more I can see the hidden connections between things, just as flying in an airplane shows me how beautifully patterned the cities and farmlands are. Civilization looks like a work of art when I am at my window seat, because I have risen above it. A smile comes over my face as I look at the world below, feeling, "I'm on top of it now . . . all this beauty and creativity."

"I'm feeling down" is also something we say, revealing our subconscious knowledge of the ladder inside.

"When I heard your tone of voice, I got that *sinking feeling* and I knew something was wrong."

I might go to the kitchen to brew some tea or do some deep breathing for a little "pick-me-up" so I can return to my work higher up the ladder than I now am. I talk about a phone call to an optimistic and funny friend of mine that "picked up my spirits." Picked UP my spirits.

When I'm in love, I'm liable not only to be as corny as Kansas in August but also as "high as a kite on the Fourth of July."

When my negative emotions have hijacked my thinking, I might say that I am "down." I'm really down. How can you laugh when you know I'm down?

Been down so long it looks like up

All the great feelings of passion and control have to do with rising, climbing higher, flying, and soaring until I am "above it all." All the weakest feelings of failure and lack of control have to do with sinking low, falling down, slipping, sliding, descending until I've "hit bottom." That is why we speak so darkly of the slippery slope.

Songwriter Richard Farina called his alternately funny and depressing autobiographical novel *Been Down So Long it Looks Like Up to Me,* whereas the song in *Space Jam,* written to honor the talent of Michael Jordan, was called "I Believe I Can Fly."

Great relationships don't come from down low in the organs. They come from high up the ladder in the imagination, as in, "Imagine me and you. I do. I think about you day and night." When both people are up in their minds and imaginations, they are happy together. The trick is to "stay up" and not get down.

When Sophia Loren was in her 60s, she was still glowing with vitality and sexuality on the movie screen. She described her formula for success by saying, "There *is* a fountain of youth—it is your mind, your talents, and the creativity you bring to life and the lives of people you love."

Sophia Loren's "mind, talents, and creativity" prescription makes no mention of clinging to someone emotionally from the heart (or any bodily organs). She had no such pre–Liz Taylor concept of using deadly grips of dependency to lock a mate into.

Seeing on the screen how great Sophia Loren looked at the end of her film career showed the proof that her system was in tune with the spirit that pervades the universe.

Hey, where are you coming from?

Your life will get better the minute you begin making it a *practice* to be aware of exactly where on the ladder you are coming from. *Practice* is the most important discovery in the history of human achievement, but in our culture, we ridicule it. We minimize its power; we try to avoid it, even though it's only practice that will give us the life we want.

The ladder is like a piano. The rungs are like keys. And practice leads to mastery.

If you can remember the ladder is there, if you can see it, then it will calm you. When you calmly see the ladder inside, you will always know which rung you are on when you are communicating or thinking.

If you notice that you are "coming from" a lower rung, such as guilt, when you are about to say something, you can step back and breathe. If you realize you are coming from anger or shame, you can take a walk and let your spirit gather the necessary lightness to ascend. Going up the ladder is much easier after deep, inspired breathing. It makes you lighter in mood, so that you can ascend more easily. (Some people claim to completely change who they are by going for a run.)

When you are hurt by what someone says, you will soon get in the habit of taking a deep breath and noticing the dynamic of it. The old habit, you'll notice, was to *stop breathing* and *feel* something about it. This shortness of breath always took you down the ladder, not up.

Once you see where you are coming from, you can then ask yourself where you *want* to come from. Who do you want to be? You invent yourself anyway, so why not reinvent upward? And if you want to create a better relationship and feel happier inside, you will want to come from higher up the ladder. You will want to come from your imagination, not your fear. You'll want to come from spirit and thoughtfulness.

With practice, you can rise up your ladder more and more often. Imagination does it. Meditation and contemplative prayer do it. And there are some physical things that can get you headed upward, too.

I like to think of LSD. It's a formula I use. "LSD" to me (now) stands for laughing, singing, and dancing. All three take you up your ladder. Laughing always gets you high on your ladder in rapid, explosive ways. (And remember to stay up. Don't laugh and come down. The higher you are, the funnier it gets. Stay with it.)

Singing, as leaders of religions know, gets you up there, too. So sing a lot. When American psychologist and religious philosopher William James realized, "We don't sing because we're happy, we're happy because we sing," he had learned the secret of the ladder. And you can dance. Dance across the planet. That's what distance runners do. They dance. That's what kids in a playground do. That's what racquetball players do, too. And notice the faces of people on the real dance floor, no matter what age! They can be the happy faces of the kids at the junior high prom dancing to Drake or Beyonce, or of the people at a senior center dancing to Paul McCartney. They are the faces of people on top of the world, on top of the ladder.

Laughing, singing, and dancing can be added to every day you live. In fact, count each day that you don't do all three as a lost day. Be strict with yourself about this. Reinvent yourself as a laugher, a singer, and a dancer. *Insist* on learning to live fully.

The happier you let yourself be, the easier life is on you.

The three activities of the LSD formula have something in common: extra *breathing* (the spirit drawn in). All three require an instant surge of breath. Laughing, singing, and dancing all take extra oxygen. To be happy? All you need is the air that you breathe. You don't have to travel with dark glasses into an inner-city crack house to score your oxygen. It's all around you.

17

No Need to Be
Queen for a Day

IT TOOK ME YEARS OF looking back to see that self-pity had
become an addiction in my life, a very nasty habit. It acted on
the system much like heroin. It hooked me into feeling numb
to life. It made creative action almost impossible.

I remember as a young man I was beginning to make my
journey back to inner strength and happiness after a lifelong
habit of self-pity. While rummaging through a used book store,
I found an old book on personal power. In the book was a little
test to see how happy you were. It asked the question, "Would
you rather be pitied or envied?" I immediately checked the box
next to "pitied." No question! Did they even have to ask?

At the time I didn't see how weak that selection was. I'm
glad I didn't; I may never have continued on my path to reinvention. Today, though, I can barely write about that choice
without feeling a lot of embarrassment.

You don't have to go as far down as I went. You can have
more fun than I did bringing your awareness to life. You can see

self-pity when it starts to set in and simply push it aside. You can make fun of yourself. You can laugh at how ridiculous you are. You are not a victim of your feelings. You are more than your feelings. Feel them. Feel them with everything you've got, and then move on up. Don't give them the last word. Get back up into, and then far beyond, your mind. Dream, laugh, reinvent, love. That's the ultimate leap reinvention makes: from fear to love.

Self-pity drives people away

One of the fastest ways to unravel a relationship is to bring self-pity into the picture.

When I catch myself being eloquent about how circumstances and other people have damaged me, I notice immediately that my relationships are losing their closeness. Suddenly people don't look forward to talking to me.

During my first 30-some years on the planet, I was a lonely, personality-obsessed victim. Even as a young boy, I thought of myself as a martyr, no matter how spoiled I was or how easy my life had become. (The odd fact is, the easier life gets, the more victimized we are likely to feel. Parents learn this the hard way. It drives them crazy. The more spoiled the child, the angrier the child. This is basically what undid the bored and angry Kurt Cobain, as even Courtney Love realized in the end.)

My favorite TV show as a sad little child was *Queen for a Day*. It was a show about victims. I spent many hours of my youth glued to my TV set as the contestants on that show told their own dark stories of how awful their lives had been. The most pathetic story always won. At the finish, the host would escort the winning woman up to the front of the stage and put a crown on her head as tears of joy rolled down her cheeks.

I remember watching how the losing contestants envied the winner and looked angry that their own stories weren't sad enough for them to have won the huge cash prize. They were not only losers in life, but losers on this show about being losers.

I remember feeling resentful at the time about not being born female. I would never be on *Queen for a Day*. That's life, I thought to myself. Life is unfair.

Later in my life, though, I was able to capture some of the *Queen for a Day* feeling when it was pointed out to me that I was a member of an officially recognized victim group. I was an "adult child of alcoholics."

"What does that mean?" I eagerly asked the person who was counseling me at the time.

"Well, because your parents were both alcoholics during your formative years, you are now an 'adult child' of alcoholics. You, in effect, are a victim of having grown up in a dysfunctional family."

"You are joking," I said joyfully. "A true victim?"

I wanted to open a bottle of champagne to celebrate.

I had previously worried that being a healthy white male growing up in Birmingham, Michigan, had left me out of any possible victim classification in our society. I was now finding out that I had been a victim and a martyr all along! At last, I was a candidate for *Queen for a Day*.

Wild thing, you make my heart sing

But "a day" was about as long as the good feelings lasted. Delving into my past and working on my childhood anger issues only served to drive me deeper into pitying myself. I was actually putting a deeper groove into my pessimistic outlook on life and people. I was polishing my story and adding more layers to my personality cocoon.

Over the years, I have found out that people will show you *some* sympathy when you pity yourself, but they don't necessarily look forward to talking to you again. (Unless they, too, are victims. Then they listen to you impatiently, waiting to get their own victim stories told.)

The great and spirited novelist D.H. Lawrence once said, "I never saw a wild thing sorry for itself. A small bird will drop dead frozen from a bough without ever having felt sorry for itself."

That's because wild things live lives of pure action. They don't have stories or personalities. Today, the more I remember to live like a wild thing, taking action instead of brooding on my sad self, the faster self-pity drops away. Chronic sadness seems to become a thing of the past. No wonder André Gide observed that sadness is almost never anything but a form of fatigue.

And fatigue, paradoxically, is almost always a result of living a life of too *little* action. The more action I build into my life, the better I sleep, and the less self-pity I feel. The better I sleep, the more energy I have. The more energy I have, the more *will* I will have for taking action, and the more action I take, the happier I feel. The happier I feel, the better my relationships. The better my relationships, the better I sleep. It's the cycle of self-reinvention.

18

Yes Lives in the Land of No

An owner is not afraid to make a request. That's why owners do so well in sales and courtship.

Victims fear the word *no* and will do amazing things to avoid ever hearing it. To a victim, "no" means rejection. Total, devastating rejection. "No" doesn't just sound like "no" to the victim, it sounds like, "No, no, NO, you are NOT WORTH ANYTHING!"

But to an owner, "no" is simply the other side of "yes." "No" and "yes" live together. Every human being has a perfect right to say either "yes" or "no" and this does not bother an owner. The owner honors that right. Therefore, when owners hear "no," they don't think something is wrong with the universe. They don't conclude that life is unfair. They move right on to their next request. Life is requests and promises.

Victims spend the better part of their lives trying to avoid hearing the word "no," because they've made it mean rejection—total, thorough, and personal—rejection. It is little wonder they want to avoid it whenever possible. The trouble is that by avoiding "no," they also avoid "yes." The two go together. They live together.

The primary reason that people don't get what they want in life is that they are afraid to ask for it. Afraid of the rejection they have made "no" to mean to themselves.

In Thomas Hardy's *Far From the Madding Crowd,* Gabriel is a victim, stuck in a made-up cocoon of a personality:

> Gabriel looked her long in the face, but the firelight being faint there was not much to be seen.
>
> "Bathsheba," he said, tenderly and in surprise, and coming closer, "if only I knew one thing—whether you would allow me to win you and love you, and marry you after all—if only I knew that!"
>
> "But you will never know," she murmured.
>
> "Why?"
>
> "Because you never ask."

High school confidential

In high school, I was so afraid of "no," I wouldn't ask anyone to the prom without knowing in advance whether she would go with me. So I would begin an elaborate and manipulative network of phone calls, trying to avoid being openly honest. I'd asked Greg to ask Patsy to ask her friend in class if she liked me enough to go out with me if I asked her to the prom even though I didn't know if I would. I was just wondering hypothetically and would like to hear back if Patsy didn't mind calling Kitty and then telling Greg so that when I called Greg again tomorrow he could tell me.

When Greg called and said, "Patsy said Kitty sort of likes you," I wasn't at all happy.

"*Sort of?*" I said. "What does that mean, Greg? That doesn't mean anything. I could call her and ask her to the prom and I could look like a complete idiot! I can just hear her now: 'Hey, look, I told Patsy to tell Greg that I liked you, but I *never said* I would *go to the prom* with you. That's a completely different thing! That guy would have to be cool. Not you.'"

There were always average-looking uninteresting guys in high school who went to dances with incredibly beautiful, fascinating dates and I never knew how they did it. None of us could figure it out. I know now. They weren't afraid of being told no. They just kept asking.

An owner of the spirit succeeds because an owner doesn't have an irrational, superstitious fear of failure. The owner wanders bravely into the land of "no." With practice.

"I've missed more than 9,000 shots in my career," said Michael Jordan. "I've lost more than 300 games. Twenty-six times I've been trusted to take the game-winning shot, and missed. I've failed over and over and over again in my life . . . and that's why I succeed."

There is a big difference between losing and being *defeated*. A victim uses losing to justify quitting the game. But an owner loses beautifully. The owner uses the loss for inspiration.

Go into your daily calendar and write "Today's Big Request" in an upper corner of the page. Don't let a single day go by without making a daring request of someone. I promise that you will be shocked at how many times you will hear an unexpected "yes!" And you will also be surprised at how well you begin to handle "no." You will learn to hear "no" with grace and humility and not take it personally anymore. By teaching yourself daily that "no" does not kill you, your power will grow far beyond your expectation. You'll feel the meaning of Nietzsche's words, "What does not kill me makes me stronger." You will look back on what was once your "personality" and laugh out loud at how far you've flown beyond that. When action replaces your personality, you have learned reinvention.

Action doesn't care about yes and no. To action, yes and no are just signposts like left and right, or up or down. They don't mean anything discouraging. The more you respect action, the faster you get what you want.

19

Love Doesn't Come From the Heart

LOVE COMES FROM A PLACE much higher on the ladder of selves than the heart. Love comes from beyond imagination. Love comes from the spirit.

Sympathy is the highest value clung to by the victim because it validates clinging to a position on the lowest rungs of the ladder. But sympathy does not achieve more than love. It should not take the place of love.

The sympathetic, commiserating person is not necessarily thoughtful. If you are present at the scene of a terrorist's bombing, and there are bleeding bodies trapped throughout a building, you are of no use to those people if you drop to your knees and start sobbing at the sight of the blood and pain. Your empathy is not an automatic good thing. In many cases, you can be more helpful (and loving) to someone if you *don't* let your emotions swamp you and you instead rise above them to a level of loving action.

"Love is not an emotion," says Deepak Chopra, "but rather it is the deep consciousness and experience of unity with the spirit."

During times of war, the medics who have saved the most lives on the battlefield were the ones who were able to rise above their feelings and access the pure energy of the spirit. Those who were most overwhelmed by sympathy for the wounded were the *least helpful* to them.

When we deal with other people, there is a way to access the pure energy of the spirit. It begins by seeing that there are basically two kinds of interpersonal communication habits: the habit of mindfully *creating* relationships and the habit of emotionally *reacting* to other people. Owners create and victims react.

A victim who gets a nasty memo will fire off a heated e-mail that, a week from now, he will regret sending. A victim lover will send back all her letters in a fit of anger. A victim board member will stalk out of a meeting saying he'll never come back. These are all reactions. With a stronger respect for action, and a lesser regard for personal ego, and more oxygen flowing into the brain, these people all might have created a better response. They might have saved the day with something more thoughtful.

The really good news is that these two methods of relating to other people—reacting and creating—*are* just habits, and because they are just habits, they can be replaced. The habit of reacting can be replaced with the habit of creating. And the first step toward replacement is awareness. If I am only emotionally reacting to you, I must first notice it and be with it. As Nathaniel Branden says, "You can't leave a place you've never been."

The sad lyric of an old country song

When I'm consulting people who are having a tough time in professional or personal relationships, it soon becomes apparent that their trouble is originating in their habit of only reacting to other people. They are turning their emotional control over to other people. Other people tick them off. Other people frustrate them. Other people intimidate them. Other people sadden them. Other people obviously control them.

Listening to their stories, I drift into a fantasy that I am hearing the lyrics of country music—songs that talk of being betrayed, of people being hurt so many times they'll never love again. Old songs with titles such as "Oh Lonesome Me," "Born to Lose," and "Is It Cold in Here or Is It You?"

The cure for a lifelong habit of emotional reaction is a fresh new burst of insight, the colorful explosion of human imagination. Plato said, "Thinking is the soul talking to itself," and if the soul gets a good conversation going, then the ride up the ladder of selves has begun.

Don't just react to this other person! Think about how you can help this other person. The action here is *service*. Don't think about what the person is doing to *you*. Only a self-obsessed ego can be wounded. Action itself can't be wounded. Spirit can't be wounded. If you are just action, serving the other person, there is no person to be wounded.

20

Please Be More
Than You Feel

IF YOU BANG YOUR KNEE on the car door getting out of the car, you really feel it. Your knee is sore. You don't deny it or repress it. You feel it. However, you also know that there is more to you than your sore knee. In fact, you can probably still go inside and do what you were going to do despite the sore knee. And if you really get enthused about what you're doing, the awareness of the sore knee disappears, and you hardly think about it again.

This is a very healthy way you relate to physical pain. You feel it and move on. Although you pay attention to it, you always know that there's more to you than the pain. You, in effect, rise above it. It's your lifelong practice to do so. It's your habit. And the habit serves you.

Now, to change your life for the better, see if you can bring the same habit to your emotional pain. If you begin today to put this same practice into effect when you feel anger, fear, guilt, or resentment, then you can become free from the feeling that other people control your moods.

In other words, you can, with practice, see that although you feel angry, you are more than the anger. Although you feel intimidated, there is more to you than that one feeling.

At first, you might experience great resistance to doing this because our entire culture has habituated us to identifying completely with our feelings. When a feeling comes along, we actually become that feeling. We *are* angry. That's what and who we are. It has consumed us entirely. Every cell in our body is angry. There is nothing more to us than this anger we are now feeling. It is accepted by everyone around us that there is nothing abnormal about saying, "I *am* angry." It is accepted practice to identify completely with the anger. The anger is who we are at that moment. It's all we are.

Yet it doesn't have to be this way. You can see a way out of this depressing habit if you think back to your sore knee and observe how you are about your knee. When you bang your knee and it hurts, you do not immediately identify with your knee. You don't walk in the house and announce, "I am a sore knee." You don't allow every cell in your body to take over that identity, as you do with your emotional pain. Why is that?

Habit.

You can adopt the same balanced, healthy, effective, and powerful habit you have with physical pain and use that habit with emotional pain. You can start today. If you feel angry, notice it and don't deny it, *but don't identify with it.* Don't let it win you over. Don't confuse it with who you really are, because it is *not* who you really are. You can say to yourself, "I feel a lot of anger about this," and localize it and box it into the context in which it deserves to fit. You can isolate it so that it can be processed, *in exactly the same way you isolate your knee's pain, and keep it in your knee.*

It is only an illusion that our emotions are who we are, that they consume us. We can check this out by handing an angry person a winning lottery ticket for $8 million. Would he say, "I can't even think about that ticket right now because I'm so angry at this person"? No. He will forget the person immediately.

If he is "depressed" sitting in a lawn chair by the pool and someone's baby falls into the water, does he say, "I wish I wasn't so depressed right now so I had the energy to jump in and save that baby!"? When the police and the paramedics write their reports, will they say that there was a witness who didn't save the child because unfortunately the witness was depressed at the time?

No, that's not what happens. You know it and I know it. We do have the power to set *any* emotion aside if there's an emergency, or a bigger game to play. But that game can be ours to imagine. We can reinvent ourselves from an emotion to an action when we get into that game.

21

We Are Either
Givers or Takers

In relationships, there are givers and there are takers. Each one is a personal invention, and each one gets a different result.

The givers have fun with other people. They are confident of their position as givers, while the takers are usually paranoid about being exposed as takers and losing the relationship.

A few years ago, I had the entertaining privilege of co-writing a book called *RelationSHIFT*. It was about raising money for good causes, and it described a "shift" that occurs in a relationship when it goes from taking to giving.

The shift that occurred was a deliberate reinvention that anyone can do. And although my co-author, Michael Bassoff, and I originally applied the concept to fund-raising, I later saw that it applied to all relationships, professional and personal. When we shift from being takers to being givers, the relationship always gets better.

Working with salespeople, I noticed that the ones who struggled the most were seeing themselves as takers. They called for an appointment and apologized for *taking* someone's time on the phone. Then they asked if they could *take* more time in person to demonstrate the product. At the demonstration, they soon got around to asking if they could *take* some of the customer's money.

It's a life of taking. So it's small and miserable.

There's nothing more depressing in relationships than feeling like you are taking more than the other person is from the relationship—feeling like you are a relationship thief. The Band sings about this pain in the Bob Dylan song "Tears of Rage": "Tears of rage / tears of grief / why must I always be a thief?"

The treasure island of giving

I love studying happy salespeople's relationships with their customers. Like Robert Louis Stevenson said, I believe that "everyone lives by selling something," and you can learn a lot from the world of sales. For one thing, the great salespeople don't see themselves as takers.

They *give* for a living.

They give their time; they give their advice; they give an offer of friendly service; they give a promise of a caretaking professional relationship. They bring a great product to the world, and see themselves as making a contribution to the lives of their customers. They glow with energy. That energy comes from the giving concept they hold of themselves.

"Self-concept," says Nathaniel Branden, "is destiny."

And so, the *givers* who work in sales prosper. The universe rewards their giving by giving back to them.

The takers, however, are weakened by their poor concept of themselves. They always feel inferior to their customers.

The shift of reinvention from being a taker to being a giver is a shift that requires action. The act of giving itself is what first activates the spirit, and soon the giver is soaring into a new dimension of life.

Most people have a hard time giving because they have misunderstood the results of previous attempts. They remember being disappointed and victimized. They don't trust giving because they think they have given before and have been burned. But they have not.

What they have called giving was actually a form of *trading*. Trading is not giving. Trading is an act that focuses on what the return will be. True giving does not focus on the return. It focuses on the giving. The giver gives without conditions, and then moves mental energy right away to the next person to give to, and never looks back.

Accomplished givers become filled with self-respect. Often, they are former takers who have reinvented themselves. They are not giving in order to get happiness in return. The happiness is already there. It lives inside the act of giving.

22

How Do You Change a Victim?

THE MOST COMMONLY ASKED QUESTION I get regarding owners and victims is, "What do you do if you have a victim in your life?"

Most people still want to change other people before they change themselves. They still don't understand that if they were high enough on their own ladder, another person being a victim would not be such a big problem. It would be an interesting situation and an opportunity for giving, but it would not be a big problem.

You will never truly reinvent yourself until other people stop being a problem to you.

If some victim in your life is still "causing" you that much of an emotional problem, you have become a victim yourself—a victim of the victim.

People can easily see victimized thinking in their spouse or their work partner. Soon they are thinking, "*That's* the problem. If *they* weren't such a *victim,* I wouldn't have such a hard time remaining an owner!"

After making sure that people understand that ownership is not about fixing other people, I usually give them my favorite Gandhi observation: "You must *be* the change you wish to see in others." Gandhi was recommending self-reinvention as the only worthy activity in the world. If we reinvent *ourselves*, that other person will want to follow us, saying, "Show me how you do that!" We must be the change we wish to see in others.

Inspiration is the strongest teaching tool ever used. One of the reasons Alcoholics Anonymous has had more success than any other method of getting people sober is because it is a program of "*attraction* rather than promotion." They don't put pressure on you to get sober. But in case you want to, AA is there to inspire you.

Parents quickly learn this tool. Children do not listen to what we say; they listen to who we are. I can tell my son to exercise all day long and he will respond with, "Yeah, right." But when I step up my own exercise program, he becomes interested, without a word from me.

Jeff Bucher, a sales manager with an office products company, has a very effective cold-calling technique that he passes on to his salespeople. But because Bucher has a deep understanding of human psychology and motivation, he does not try to *teach* his method to his people, he *inspires* them with it. When one of his people is struggling with cold-calling, Bucher hops in the car and says, "Let's go call on some people," and then he personally demonstrates his system.

Give up: I'm right, you're wrong

The worst way to communicate in a relationship is to make someone wrong about something. The minute my communication has you thinking you're wrong, I've put you on the defensive, and real communication has been replaced by the need to survive.

When I make you wrong, your first reaction is to defend yourself. And then by defending yourself, you become more convinced that you're right. The more convinced you are, the less likely you are to change.

So by criticizing other people, we are *increasing* the behavior that we object to. Not a very effective way to build good relationships. Even if we say to ourselves that we are being "constructive" in our criticism, we are not. All criticism that makes someone feel wrong and defensive is destructive.

So if there's a victim in our lives, the worst thing we can do is make him or her feel wrong for being a victim.

The best thing we can do is ignore the victimized thinking and wait in the bushes for an ownership moment. No one is a total victim. Everyone has moments of pure optimism and spirit. The trouble is, when those moments show up, we usually highlight them in the worst possible way. We usually comment on how rare the moment is.

"Well, where did *that* come from!" we say. "That's not the Michael *I* know. Did you have a religious conversion or something? I'm usually the one who recommends these things, not you. I'm the one who has to always show us the bright side, not you. To what do we owe this rare and unusual moment? What have I done to deserve your first positive thought of the new year?"

By highlighting the rarity of the thought, we *discourage* our victim from thinking that way again.

The most effective treatment of a rare ownership moment is to really reward it, and in a sincere way, that encourages the victim to come up with another one soon.

When the victims in my life share an ownership moment with me, I like to slow down time. I like to stop the clock altogether if I can and really enjoy the moment. I like to tell other people about the victim's ownership thinking, and refer back to it in the days ahead. I like to do as much with it as I can so that the victim begins to look for more ownership thoughts to create.

We don't have to wait until a victim changes into an owner. A victim is already an owner. The problem is in the frequency of expression of ownership. Once we get good at honoring that expression, the moments will increase. The more we can relax about who the victim is, the more freedom that person has to experiment. Soon, the victim's old personality disappears and they learn to be strong.

So, how do you change a victim?

See the owner in them.

Stop making them wrong.

23

Forgiveness Is a Mother

AFTER LOSING MY TEMPER WITH a young woman who had not prepared a seminar room properly for one of my courses, I sat alone at my desk and thought about what I had done. I'd given her a stern lecture on professionalism, taking responsibility, and customer relations, and I was hopping mad at her. And even though everything I was talking about was "justified," I wondered why I was so emotionally upset about it. I asked myself, if a *man* had made the same mistakes, would I have become so furious?

And to my discomfort, I had to answer no. In fact, a similar event had occurred a few weeks prior when one of our young men who works in customer relations had sent out the wrong dates to clients about some upcoming seminars. When I saw him in the hallway the next day, I playfully pretended to be surprised and said, "Are you still working here?" He laughed and apologized for the mistake, and I took some time to explain to him how important the correct information was. He got the point and it never happened again.

Sitting at my desk and reviewing that incident, I realized that I experienced no fury or rage. I wondered if the difference was that it was a man and not a woman.

I immediately talked to Steve Hardison, my coach and mentor, about this problem. He suggested that until I forgave my mother for whatever it was I was still angry with her about, I would never relate to women in the exact same way I related to men.

"My *mother?*" I asked him.

Then I began to reconsider my problem. "But I don't treat all women that way," I protested. And I proceeded to list a number of women I admired and respected and treated well.

"That's true," he said, "but think of how hard they had to work to earn your respect. And you give that respect immediately to a man just because he's a man."

I knew he was right. So, reluctantly, I began to think about my mother.

I was of two minds about my mother. Originally, my mother was the most beautiful and loving person I had ever known, and my first years on the planet were spent idolizing her. (My father was still away from home in the army fighting in World War II.)

But as the years rolled on, my mother began her descent into alcoholism and addiction to tranquilizers. At the time, I had no idea what was going on. Her daily change of mood and personality terrified me. Each day, after lunch, for some mysterious, dark reason, she became sloppy, stupid, and mean right before my eyes. It never improved. In fact, even though I was a little boy, I could tell that it was getting worse and worse.

I believe I never really got over that shock to my system, and I also believe that I made some kind of subconscious conclusion that *women* were that way. All of them. They were not to be trusted.

Are all women like my mother?

After thinking a little more about this issue, I called Devers Branden, a consultant in California and the wife of author Nathaniel Branden. I had written extensively in a previous book about the many great things Devers's advice and coaching had done for me in my life, and now I knew I needed her help again.

"I think I need to forgive my mother," I told her. "I don't think I have ever forgiven my mother, and I know it's influencing my relationships with women. Because of how my mother behaved toward me during her addictions, I think I stored up a tremendous sense of anger and betrayal that I have never forgiven her for. And now I don't think I grant women the same trust I grant to men, and it's much harder for a woman to win my respect. I know that's not right. I hate that about myself, and I never really saw it until now. I need to find a way to forgive my mother."

Devers was as gentle, intelligent, and strong as I had expected. The first thing she did was suggest that we drop the whole idea of "forgiving." The very word, "forgiving," she pointed out, suggests that a sin has been committed by my mother. That she had deliberately committed a sin against me, that I was right and my mother was wrong, and that I was a victim.

Devers suggested that we look for something stronger and more permanent than forgiveness, something like complete acceptance—the complete realization that my mother lived the only way she saw possible, given how she saw the world, and that I probably would have done the same thing if I'd had the same life experiences, fears, and dreams as my mother, that it wasn't directed at me in any way. Total acceptance. (Not approval, just acceptance.) I realized that I was not an intended victim. I was not the target. And that "forgiveness" would just deepen the idea that a mighty wrong had taken place. That I had been sinned against.

She immediately asked me to talk to her about what I loved most about my mother. I really surprised myself as I went on and on in such detail about how loving my mother was and how she gave up alcohol late in life and courageously lived her final years as a completely optimistic single woman, reinventing all her relationships with her children. I said that every impulse I have ever felt to love another person and love my children came from my mother. She was love itself.

I began to feel all my anger toward my mother melting away. The more I talked to Devers, the more I accepted the whole person that my mother was. I actually achieved what Devers had first recommended: a state of acceptance that went way beyond forgiveness.

Steve Hardison agreed that Devers was right: "I can see what she means. When we say we *forgive* someone, we are still implying that we are morally superior to them—that they have done us wrong and we will condescend to forgive them for it. By doing that, we still get to be victims."

I was beginning to feel really great. I made a strong commitment to myself to be very aware of how I think about women from now on, and to practice opening my mind to them whenever it starts to close. I thought I had finished some important new work, but I was not finished.

"One more thing to do," said my coach, Hardison. "Now you must call all the women in this company together and tell them everything you have been through in the past few days. Tell them everything, and ask if they will help you on your path to total acceptance."

I was shocked and stunned by the idea. Hardison always has a way of doing that. He finds the fastest and most dramatic way to shock someone's system into complete change.

I couldn't imagine doing what he wanted me to do. It was just too embarrassing. So I tried to get out of it. I told him I'd try to do it one at a time. That I'd meet with each woman in the company individually. It would be more "meaningful" that way.

He reluctantly agreed. But when, after two weeks, I had met with only one woman, he changed the plan. He has a bias for action.

"Let's just do it," he said. "And I'll sit in the meeting with you to lend you support."

I agreed to do it, and when the day came and I found myself sitting in a circle of more than 10 women and Hardison, I felt huge butterflies in my stomach. But I started to talk, and as soon as I did, I knew this was the right thing. As hard as it was, I knew I was putting my past behind me for good.

I talked about my mother and my new commitment and I asked for help. I was amazed at the response. The women in the company went around the room taking time to talk to me and support me. Many of the women said they had the same problem with men—that they were afraid of men in some way because of their fathers. I was really moved by the experience.

I found myself wishing that my mother had been there. And then I realized that in many ways, she was there.

Reinvention involves growing up. Growing above and beyond the hurts and memories of the past so that other people have a clean slate with you. Reinvention involves letting go of judgments about people in your past. It isn't the memory that hurts you, it's the judgment that the memory is about something that was "wrong."

The more I feel that I've been "done wrong" in the past, the less there is of me to do right in the future.

Part Three

Life and Death Sentences

It is good to be happy; it's a little better to know
that you're happy; but to understand that you're
happy and know why and how . . . and still be
happy, be happy in the being and the knowing,
well that is beyond happiness, that is bliss.

—Henry Miller
Colossus of Maroussi

24

Words Can Be Stronger Than Drugs

THE HIGH SCHOOL KIDS WERE hunched over and vomiting behind the bleachers at the football game.

Was it a reaction to a drug? No. It was a reaction to some words being spoken! They were having a stomach-wrenching physical reaction to an announcement made on the public address system at the game that the Coke machine was defective and the soft drinks had been contaminated, and that there were other kids who had just been taken to the hospital.

However, the tests at the hospital weren't complete. When they were, the doctors realized that the first few kids who had come in had all been to the same restaurant where they had eaten the same food that gave them food poisoning. All those other sick kids did not have food poisoning. They didn't have anything wrong with them. It was just a hysterical chain reaction. The Coke machine was fine. False alarm.

And yet the vomiting and sickness were "real." The vomiting had now spread to both sides of the field. And it was caused by the *words* coming over the P.A. system.

I can watch the same phenomenon inside myself when I choose one sentence over another. When I come home from work tired and worn out, I can think to myself, "Man, am I ever tired. I really don't want any hassle from my kids. I just want to vegetate. I'm exhausted." Those words will have a definite effect on the animating force within me.

Or I can breathe myself a little higher up the ladder toward the spirit and I can say, "Pleasantly tired as I am, I love this life of mine, and my kids are fun. They are a welcome distraction after a day on the job. They are here to amuse and delight me. I will honor my pleasant fatigue and still enjoy all the little light moments and absurdities of family life. I will laugh. I may even dance."

The choice for me is always there. I can own my thinking, or be a victim of my thoughts. Victims experience thoughts as things that *happen to* them, as if the thoughts were transmitted from Roswell, New Mexico.

Owners guide the patterns of their thoughts. (Thinking begins with chosen phrases and sentences, and those words then paint the pictures that fire the spirit.)

Pessimism is literally sickening

There are many other studies that prove that words and thoughts are stronger than drugs. Some are cited by Michael Talbot in *The Holographic Universe*. His book notes the evidence that "people with AIDS 'who display a fighting spirit' live longer than AIDS-infected individuals who have a passive attitude. People with cancer also live longer if they maintain a fighting spirit. Pessimists get more colds than optimists. Stress lowers the immune response. People who score high on tests designed to measure hostility and aggression are seven times more likely to die from heart problems than people who receive low scores."

Talbot also cites the study that showed that the mental attitude an expectant mother has toward her baby, and pregnancy in general, has a direct correlation with the complications she will experience during childbirth, as well as with the medical problems her newborn infant will have after he or she is born. Her mental attitude begins with the habitual words and phrases she uses. If she has wonderful *challenges* and *opportunities* in her life, her life is full of optimism and good health. If she has nothing but *problems* and *trouble,* then she feels weak in the morning and tired by the evening. She thinks she's *describing* her situations with the word *problems*, but she's actually creating them.

The examples go on and on.

An inspired manager at Texas Instruments, where my partner Dennis Deaton and I had been teaching our courses on ownership, came up with the idea of outlawing the word "they" in his team meetings. As in, "why do *they* want us to do that? Why can't *they* see our problems? What kind of pricing are *they* going to make us work with now? Why won't *they* give us better parking?" From now on, just for fun, the team would declare that "they" was as inappropriate as the "F" word.

And you might wonder, what real difference could that make? After all, "they" is just a word. But it was remarkable how much of the us-versus-them thinking disappeared when "they" was replaced by "we" in the workplace.

The French have a saying: "He who is absent is always wrong." This saying is insightful. Notice how the person who is not there is usually the one likely to be talked about disparagingly. If someone is not *there* to explain themselves, *they* are the ones who get to be wrong. When the word "we" took the place of "they," there was less antagonism, less alienation, and less resentment of other people in other departments.

And it was just a word.

Previously, the employees were using "they" all the time: "They won't let us do that," or "They don't pay me enough to do that," or "They don't understand us."

Now they were saying, "Why do *we* have this policy?"

And when employees heard it that way, their next thought was, "Let's get together to talk about this."

The Texas Instruments manager had such success with that one-word replacement that he had buttons made up with the word "they" on them with a red circle around the word and a red line diagonally through it.

By altering the words and sentences we use when we talk to ourselves and others, we alter our experience of life. We can learn to step back to see how we are literally "sentencing" ourselves to the lives we live.

"Why do *we* have this policy?" is a much stronger question than "Why are *they* making us do this?" The first question creates an owner, and the second creates a victim.

Are they pigs or blue knights?

Listen to your language as you go through your day. Pay close attention to the word "they" as it comes up. It could be an opportunity to substitute it with "we" for a stronger experience of life.

These self-victimizing thinking habits start early. I was driving along a remote dirt farm road with my children recently outside of Gilbert, Arizona, and we pulled up to a stop sign in the middle of nowhere. My children began to scornfully ask, "Why did they put a stop sign way out here?"

"We put it here," I said.

"What?"

"*They* didn't put it here, *we* did."

"What do you mean, Dad?"

"We create our cities and towns. We do. We vote for people who choose people who make these decisions. We call our representatives when we don't like something, and we fix it. We drive on one side of the road because we've agreed to, so we won't hurt each other. We agree to stop at a red light. It's our system. All of this is our idea. The police some people call pigs are people who *we* have hired with our own hard-earned money. They work for us. They are not against us, and they are not separate from us. We create society. There is no society apart from us. We put that stop sign there. We had a reason."

My children had grown silent. Finally Bobby said, "Is this one of your seminars, Dad? If it is, it's great but. . . ." Perhaps I hadn't yet persuaded them that there isn't some alien "they" out there conspiring against us to make life miserable.

Each time you notice yourself using "they," see if "we" would be a more powerful way to see things. After a few switches from one word to the other, you'll be delighted with your new word habit and how it opens your world up. You'll be like James Bond with a new gadget. You'll look for opportunities to use it all the time.

Reinvention begins at the level of thought. Don't let your thoughts think you. Step back and witness your thoughts.

Watch them flying by one after the other. Notice the effect your thoughts have on your feelings. Now gently guide them to where you want them to go. And, remember: Sometimes it's good not to think at all. To take time out and give it a rest. No mind. No thought.

Reinvention often comes faster from no thought than from thought. Allow some form of meditation or contemplative prayer to center you regularly. Close your eyes often, so that your brain can go to the alpha brain wave state more often and out of agitated beta all day. Give it a rest. Then rise up. The new you.

25

How We Sentence Ourselves

OUR ENERGY AND MOOD ARE created by the language we think
with. The language impact is stronger than drugs, as medical
tests with placebos have revealed for years. ("One pill makes
you larger. The other makes you small." Whatever the doctor
says about the pill actually influences what the pill seems to do.)

I could now see that my own work with high and low
achievers had taught me exactly the same thing: People who
are productive and fulfilled in life use a different language
than the people who are struggling.

I'd even gotten to the point where I could interview people
without knowing in advance if they were performing well or
not, and I was able, just by listening to their language, to tell.
Some of my clients began to joke that it was a psychic ability, but I told them it was different (partly because I needed
to charge more than psychics do). I said I was just listening to
their words.

You can always tell where a person's *from* by listening to the language he or she uses. Some people come from ownership, and some from victimization.

I began keeping notebooks filled with the language of high achievers (who I labeled "owners") and another bulging pile of notebooks filled with the language of the people who were frustrated and struggling (the "victims").

Owners used the words "I can" a lot, while victims favored "I can't." Owners had goals, projects, and challenges, whereas victims had problems, hassles, and nightmares. Owners said they were busy, and victims said they were swamped. Owners were "designing a life" while victims were "trying to make a living." Owners were psyched and excited about changes in the workplace while victims were worried and ticked off. Owners looked to see what they could get *from* an experience while victims tried to get *through* it. Owners would plan things and victims would wish things.

This link I'd seen between language and performance was interesting, but what was even more exciting was how people's lives would change once they began practicing using new language. Problems became *projects*. Jobs became *professions*. Managers became *leaders*. People began to experience a freedom that went beyond personality: a freedom to reinvent their own reality.

We don't have permanent personalities, we have shifting patterns of thought. And patterns can be interrupted and finally replaced with other patterns. In baseball there are some hitters who can hit as easily from the right side of the plate as from the left. That wasn't natural. It wasn't who they were. No one is born that way. But they put new patterns in place and became switch hitters, now effortlessly and gracefully hitting with power and precision from either side of the plate.

How do they do that? How do they do what's not natural? What happens? It's called Pattern Replacement. You can replace any pattern of behavior (or thought) with another. All it takes is relentless practice. You are not stuck. I am not stuck. We are not lost in the fabrication of who we are.

I'll never forget the moment that this first became perfectly clear to me. It was one of those moments of realization that you never forget. Business consultant Becky Robbins was teaching a course in communication, and she casually said something that tied together and clarified for me the nearly 11 years of work I had done in human development.

"Some people use language," she said, "to *describe* the lives they lead, and other people use language to *create* the lives they lead."

Yes, that was it exactly! Behind every action is a thought, formed in words that paint a picture. This felt like a new discovery to me, but I knew it wasn't new to everyone. It has since been pointed out to me that it was written long ago that "in the beginning there was the word."

26

Get Through It or Get From It

IN HIS SOPHOMORE YEAR IN high school, Michael Jordan was cut from the basketball team.

Like any kid who wanted to play basketball would be, he was depressed and angry. He wasn't good enough to play high school basketball? He totally disagreed, but the coach was the coach. However, Michael Jordan also had a habit of thinking things through, of not just walking away like a victim. He finally asked himself an owner's question: How can I use this? How can I *use* this?

He wanted to know what he could get *from* the experience. He did not ask himself how he would get *through* it.

After thinking it over, he decided to practice harder than he ever had before. He would not be defeated by the thoughts in someone else's head. In fact, not only would he make the team next year, he decided that he'd take his game to an entirely new level. It wasn't long before he took his game to a level it never would have gone to had he not been cut. Today, he discusses being cut from his high school team as a defining moment in his life—something that drove him to reinvent who he was as a player—one of *the best things that ever happened to him.*

In 1980, Candy Lightner's daughter was killed by a drunk driver in Sacramento, California. The driver was never punished. So, it might have been understandable if Candy had become a lifelong victim of this circumstance. But she decided to channel her outrage into something useful, so she started Mothers Against Drunk Driving. She refused to be the driver's second victim. She took herself up from *get through* to *get from.*

The primary result of the habit of using self-victimizing language, such as "get through," is fatigue, both mental and physical. A life that you have to get *through* is by its very nature an ongoing struggle. The air itself becomes a wall of clear, thick Jell-O to get through. You can feel it in your walk—the struggle—the unbearable thickness of being.

Whatever gets you through the night

The victims' sense of fatigue eventually leads to low performance and depression. People who are run down soon become accident-prone. Bad things start happening to them. They become incredibly unlucky. Their low state of energy robs them of the strength to get *through* their challenges. When feeling low, they stop paying attention.

They trip over a rollerblade left on the stairs—they miss half a day's work. They leave their briefcase on the roof of their car and drive off into rush hour traffic with all their notes and documents flying in the wind like huge sad confetti—it takes a week to get all their important papers and cards duplicated. They wake up late the next morning and take the wrong turn off the freeway, driving into a neighborhood where their life is threatened. They see a doctor to get a prescription to handle the increased stress and depression—soon a nasty addiction sets in.

They start beginning their sentences with the words, "With my luck. . . ." They are victims of their own thinking.

On the other hand, it is a refreshing and energizing life that is begun by trying to get something *from* everything you do. There's a shift in energy when the words are shifted.

Sometimes great songwriters and singers go through periods in their lives when they compound their self-victimization by addictions to drugs and alcohol. You can often hear the pain of these life periods in the words of their songs. Kris Kristofferson's "Help Me Make It Through the Night" and John Lennon's "Whatever Gets You Through the Night" illustrate this weariness of the spirit. Both songwriters, later in their careers, reinvented themselves. Their later songs reflect it.

For example, in *Mr. Holland's Opus*, Richard Dreyfuss sang the song John Lennon had written to his "beautiful boy." It was a song of joy. John Lennon lived his last years as an owner of the human spirit, a life in which he could "imagine all the people, living to be free." He had become, in the strongest sense, a dreamer. He had developed what Colin Wilson calls "the strength to dream." Lennon sang, "You may call me a dreamer."

You always have two ways to respond to any difficult circumstance: as an owner or as a victim. When you are confronted with difficulty, stop and think of those two options. Make sure you are paying attention to how you are describing things to yourself. If you're wondering how you're going to get *through* some experience, ask yourself to breathe a little more deeply and translate your language into that of an owner. Just try it on, as if you were trying on a baseball cap that you were thinking of purchasing. Put it on frontwards, then put it on backwards.

Try saying to yourself, perhaps even out loud as you're getting started, "How can I use this? What can I get *from* this experience? What is the gift inside of this? What is it here to teach me?"

If you listen carefully enough to your problem, you'll begin to get things from it. You will no longer want to get through it. Soon it will no longer even be thought of as a "problem." It will become your teacher.

Problems then become turning points for you. Soon you are using them and loving them (in retrospect) like an architect inventing a city, turning a street here, and a building there. People will notice that you have changed. They may call you a dreamer. But you're not the only one.

27

Cure Your Intention Deficit Disorder

THERE IS ONE WORD THAT does more damage and creates more victims than any other. It is the word "should." And you should never use it! (Oh my gosh I just did. I should be more careful.)

"Should" actually *reduces* your motivation every time you use it. "Should" is the most self-defeating word in the English language. It's like a tranquilizer to the spirit.

When I tell myself I "should" do something, I am actually reducing the chances that I'll do it. (This goes for the variations "ought to," "supposed to," obligated to," and "they're gonna get me if I don't.")

One of the reasons why "should" doesn't work as an energizer is its profoundly judgmental and unfriendly nature. I would never use the word "should" with a friend. I would never say, "Hi, Fred. How's it going? Hey man, you should lose some weight!"

If a victim is sitting at his desk on a Friday, trying to get the paperwork and forms finished before going home, he will probably, out of habit, try to motivate himself with the word "should."

"I should really get this work done," he'll say, in a depressed tone of voice. "I really ought to do it. I know I'm supposed to. Any organized person would have done it by now. Why do I always do this? Why do I always put things off? Must be my personality."

If someone comes by the victim's desk at this point, the victim is very vulnerable because he's put himself in such a distracted state with the word "should." In a way, he's been sitting there "shoulding" all over himself. The first person to come by and say, "Hey, let's go out for a beer. It's Friday. What are you, a workaholic?" pulls the victim off his task.

The victim gladly goes for the beer. The paperwork is stuffed into a huge, cluttered and deep desk drawer, and the victim is out the door.

What has just happened is the power of language at work. The victim has just lowered his own energy level with the word he was using.

The cure for chronic victim fatigue

Across the aisle from the above-mentioned victim sits an owner. She is doing her paperwork quickly and with focused energy. Inside her head, there are different words being used for inspiration. "*I want to* get this paperwork done," she says.

Does she love paperwork? No. She may hate it even more than the victim does. But she loves having it done. She loves having it out of her mind.

"I want to put it behind me," she says with increased spirit. "I want to have a weekend completely free of worry. I don't want to take my job home with me. I want to drive in Monday morning knowing my desk is clear and I have a fresh start at the new week."

Words are a lot like drugs. They operate in the brain in a remarkably similar way. Where the victim is unintentionally taking a tranquilizer ("I should"), the owner is taking a breath of fresh oxygen ("I want to").

When you are doing something because you want to, you are doing it with a different spirit. You can set yourself on fire and burn through all of your work. You consume what's in front of you with a happy vengeance.

When a victim is doing something because he "should," he is doing it resentfully and reluctantly (if he's doing it at all). He is trying to drive his car, but there is always one foot on the brake.

Because of the results of the internal language he uses, the victim sees himself as a procrastinator. Then he wonders how that trait became a part of his personality. Then, by believing that procrastination is a permanent part of his permanent personality, he never changes. How could he? It's a part of *who he is!*

But procrastination is only a temporary pattern of behavior. It is not a part of anyone's personality. It's an option. It's open to anyone anytime.

Suicide is not painless

Suicide is so tragic and serious that even the slightest irreverence about it can be startling, as when Woody Allen said, "I saw my ex-wife on the street the other day and I didn't recognize her with her wrists closed."

Language is a matter of life and death. Life and death issues are at stake in how we talk to ourselves. Repeated use of the word "should" eventually leads to depression. Depression can sometimes lead to suicide.

Even when it doesn't, we know about the *living death* we experience when we're fatigued by the repeated thought that we are living a life different than the life we "should be" living.

When you look for opportunities to shift your language from "I should" to "I want to," you'll notice that it's a life-giving shift. The spirit you connect to when you do it is the life force itself, because you are no longer resisting what is real. You're accepting it and owning it and letting it in.

Understanding and mastering how you speak to yourself is the most important project you could ever take on. Get hooked on it like a hobby. Make it an enjoyable avocation instead of a grim "change" you "should" make.

It's not always easy to mentally convert what you should be doing to "what I want to do." If you're in the habit of thinking of yourself as a weary martyr who *should* be doing things, living the life you *want* to live is like learning to swim for the first time.

But the swimming is good. It is not selfish to live the life you want. Your fear of becoming selfish is something you'll lose with practice, because you'll see how many people you benefit when you're doing things because you *want to* do them. You will feel reinvented. And your happiness will make other people happy. How can that be selfish?

I want to, I need to, I love to

At one point in my own life, I realized and admitted that I was doing the things I really wanted to do, so it didn't serve me to keep talking to myself like I was a victim: "Oh no, I have to be at work. I hate this. Why do I have to work? I guess I should be more motivated, but I'm not."

That kind of habitual language always caused my energy to leak away. And it was only a habit. It was never based on fact. It was based on habitual self-talk. The fact is, when I thought about it, I *wanted* to work! (All I had to do was think back to a time when I was out of work and longed for a job.) And I *wanted* to be on time. Why not say it?

Even if you want to change jobs or change professions, you still want to be at work on time today because you know that you enhance your prospect of getting a better job by being successful where you are.

Saying "I want to" is hard at first, but only because you're not in the habit. So you might have to fake it till you make it: "This is what I want to do! This is my choice!"

After a while, it will start to feel more real, and you'll access your energy faster and faster each morning. You'll be inventing an owner's voice inside you. All it takes is practice.

Your victim voice will actually grow weak from neglect. The less you use it, the stranger it will feel when it speaks up. Soon, the victim voice will feel "sick," and out of place. Just as when you have a cold, you know you're not quite right. You know the bad feeling is temporary and dysfunctional. You can have the victim voice be just like that.

Continue to allow yourself throughout the day to see that you're doing what you're doing *because you want to*.

Instead of moaning that you have to shovel the snow outside, you can talk internally about what you want. Think about the clean sidewalk. Think about what you want, not what you don't want. Talk to yourself about the good feeling you get in the cold fresh air when the task is complete and your muscles are pleasantly humming and the snow is all shoveled.

You want that, you know you do. So accept it. Let it in. You are already happy, deep down inside, so accept it. Let it be real. It's not going to kill you or keep you from solving life's problems if you're happy. In fact, it will help you. Happy people have more creative energy. Nobel laureate Albert Schweitzer once observed, "Success is not the key to happiness. Happiness is the key to success."

Be aware of how much you truly enjoy every journey to a goal, even small ones, like the goal of a clean walkway after a snowstorm. Let yourself know how much you enjoy it. Each shovel full. Thinking you do it because you "should" or because you "have to" is just an old habit of moping around like a victim. It often starts in childhood. It's a carry-over from underdeveloped positive emotions. Don't keep it up all your life. Your life is about evolving! Building on the good . . . keeping the best and moving on. Being a victim got you sympathy sometimes, but it didn't get you the life you wanted.

In fact, the sympathy you got probably led you to even more self-pity, and the downward spiral continued into truly depressing fatigue. I once heard the priest Father Jack Spaulding deliver a sermon on self-pity during which he yelled out to his congregation, "Get off the cross; we need the wood!"

That wood he was talking about is something you can build things with. Build a life, don't try to make a living. Reinvent yourself from someone to whom things happen, to someone who builds.

28

Honey, We Shrunk Our Daughter

A MOTHER WHO IS A victim will be in the habit of always focusing on what's *wrong* with the people in her life.

She is projecting her own internal anxiety on others. She feels bad inside, so she looks outside for a "cause" to pin that feeling on. That way, she never has to reinvent. She never has to travel inward and grow strong and new, she just projects.

So when her daughter gets good grades in everything but math, she can't stop talking about the math. When the family goes to a picnic with other family members and this mother is asked how Jennifer is doing, she says, "Oh pretty well! All her grades were quite good except for math. Right, honey?" she smiles at her daughter. "We're going to have to work on the math. We're very concerned about her math."

Someone at the picnic joins the conversation midway and says, "Jennifer's doing well in school?"

And Jennifer looks at her mother and says, in a shy voice, "Except for math."

"Yes," her mother says. "We're very worried about her math. I don't know whether we'll be doing summer school or using a tutor."

Soon, Jennifer's entire self-image is focused on her trouble in math. Who Jennifer becomes to herself and to her mother is someone who is having trouble with math. Like Kevin Costner's movie character took the name "Dances With Wolves," Jennifer might as well take the name "Trouble With Math." Soon we don't even remember what her real name is or her good subjects were. She might have gotten an A in a particularly challenging English course, but that no longer has any reality to Jennifer because her mother is obsessed with her failure in math.

Without knowing it, Jennifer's mother has actually reduced the chances that Jennifer will improve in math. In fact, what Jennifer's mother is doing is pretty much guaranteeing that Jennifer will spend the rest of her life seeing herself as a girl named "Trouble With Math."

The laziest thing the mind can do

Jennifer's mother doesn't do this because she is evil and wants to hurt Jennifer. She does it because she is projecting. Victims project their inadequacies on others.

Listen to victims speak, and it's always about other people, and how disappointing they are.

All victims do this all day long. It takes no imagination, no courage, and no energy to do it. It is the default mechanism of the human mind, just as weeds are the default mechanism of the garden.

If Jennifer's mother were to know that she is an owner of the human spirit, she would talk about Jennifer's *good* grades everywhere she went. She would realize that what we focus on grows. Even if someone asked about Jennifer's math, she would say, "Math is coming; it's on its way to being great like the others. She's going to be great at math because no one can get an A in an English class as hard as that one and not be able to absolutely do anything she wants in school."

Now Jennifer would have the freedom to play around with doing a little better at math. There is no pressure. There is nothing wrong. There is nothing wrong with Jennifer! Imagine Jennifer living in a world where there is nothing wrong with Jennifer.

Victim mothers and fathers are always drawn to their children's shortcomings, because they are always projecting their own. A criticism is a projectile.

Seeing other people's faults is the easiest thing we do. It can be done with very little thinking. But it's a habit that ends up damaging all our relationships.

Is Jennifer herself ruined by having a mother like this? Will she become depressed and try to take shortcuts to happiness for the rest of her life? No, not necessarily. Jennifer is free to invent herself in any direction she wants. But she's beginning with something that feels like a disadvantage.

For Jennifer to invent herself as an owner she will have to learn for herself how the mind and spirit work. But that's fine, because we all have to do that anyway. No matter how good the parenting was, this owner-victim thing has to be learned on your own. In the end, whether we put our energy into victim or owner, we must experience that as a choice to have any happiness at all. Happiness is in the energy choice.

Psychiatrist Peter Breggin says, "If a person has the energy—the vitality—to become 'manic' or 'depressive,' then he or she also has the energy to live an extraordinarily rich and satisfying life."

When a child's attention has been repeatedly directed at "what's wrong with me?" it is very easy for the child not to enter adult life with a feeling of "I'm not good enough."

However, in my workshops and ownership coaching I see, almost daily, people who completely liberate themselves from their self-image formed in childhood. I see people who decide to leave their personalities behind and build a life based on what's right with them, not what's wrong.

Don't continue to shrink yourself

If you were shrunk as a child, don't carry the work forward. Don't continue to shrink yourself. Don't pretend you are weaker than you are. As Nelson Mandela once said in a speech to his nation, "There is nothing enlightened about shrinking so that other people won't feel insecure around you."

The first step is total acceptance of the fact that your parents and guardians did the best they knew how and were only motivated by concern for your future. Blaming them only deepens your self-invention as a victim. Understanding your parents and the effects of their words on you is the way to gain freedom from them.

The second step is to revise your estimate of yourself based on the facts, not on hurt feelings. Study and highlight what's good. Build on your actual strengths. And when you see something in you that's weak, look at it as a welcome opportunity for new growth and adventure. Happiness comes from growth, not comfort. So why be sad about a chance to grow?

Don't get hooked into the habit of sadness about your past. It's easy to do. Sadness is an addiction. It is almost identical to an addiction to tranquilizers. Watch Glenn Close play Sunny von Bulow in *Reversal of Fortune* to see what addiction to tranquilizers does to the human spirit and demeanor.

Addiction to sadness mimics that addiction to chemical "downers" exactly. It's a version of the same downer—the same slow, low moaning in the speech, the same sluggish and weary demeanor.

If you look in the mirror and see any form of this sadness, make a decision to notice it and let it embrace you. Do not resist. It's just an invention anyway. Then, once it bores you because you've let so much of it express for so long, invent a new part to play. Give yourself a fresh start in this fresh moment. You will notice that if you don't try to resist the negative, it will pass right away on its own. Your mind has an automatic refresh button.

You can ask, "If all the world were a stage, and I were playing a part, is this really who I would want to be?" Then, invent who it is that you really want to be. Take the actions that person would take. Just for fun. Just to reinvent.

Reinvention is about options. You have options. When it comes to who you want to be in any circumstance, you have options. Exercise your options.

29

I'm Sorry, but I Was Swamped

VICTIMS CONSTANTLY USE THE WORD "swamped." But "swamped" exists only in the mind. It's a word. And the first step in draining the swamp is to pull the plug on the word.

Victims say, "I'm sorry I couldn't make it to our daughter's graduation, but I was swamped." They say, "Honey, I'm not going to be coming home when I said I would because I'm swamped."

"Swamped" is a word they use to describe a feeling. It's a feeling brought about by overwhelmed thinking. It's a word they use with other people to get them to pity and appreciate their stressful situation.

"I understand what you're saying, Steve," said an auto parts store manager to me. "But what if you're *really* swamped?"

"There's no such thing as swamped," I said. "You are not swamped until you say you are. 'Swamped' is just a word you are applying to a feeling about a situation."

"Right!" he said. "But in our work . . . if you had my job . . . I just think you'd be swamped, too."

147

I gave him an example:

"What if someone was working at one of your competitor's auto parts stores, and he didn't enjoy it. He was bored a lot on the job. And he came to work for your company. And the first morning on the job he really loved it. He was busier than he'd ever been, and the time was flying by. He was rushing around helping customers, and when the lunch hour came, he had to be told to take a break. At the break he called his wife and said, 'This is the best job I've ever had. Time just flies by here. I'm doing all kinds of things, giving advice, working for people, making decisions. I love it.'

"Now what if this man had the misfortune after his lunch hour of working next to his manager? And his manager began complaining about the store, and saying how overburdened and overwhelmed they were. How *swamped* they were today and how the corporate office never gives them enough staff to handle the customer flow, or enough parts to last a week. When our new man gets home at night and his wife asks if the afternoon was as much fun as the morning was, he is likely to say, 'No, unfortunately not. In the afternoon, we were swamped.'"

Your autopsy will not show it

There is no swamped until you say there is. If you were to die from this condition you are calling "swamped," they would not find it in you. When they put you on the table in the morgue, there would be no 'swamped' in your body. That's because swamped does not exist in life, it just exists in language.

"So what does an owner (versus a victim) say when he's swamped?" the manager asked.

"An owner is not swamped to begin with," I said. "The owner is almost always *focused*."

Focused is the opposite of swamped. An owner knows that he can only do one thing at a time, and in order to do that thing quickly and expertly, he must not be preoccupied. He must not be trying to do a million things at once and not doing anything well.

The workshops and coaching I do are sometimes delivered to people whose corporations have just undergone "downsizing," where employees have been abruptly laid off.

The bitter resentment against management is in the air during these workshops, and, fortunately, participants usually have the courage to speak up.

"What if you have fewer people in your department and you're being asked to do more?" is a common question. "What if your manager gives you more than you can do? Can't you be swamped then? Haven't you ever been up to your ass in alligators with no way to drain the swamp?"

Yes, I have. But it was *my own thinking* that had me up to it with alligators. Someone in the habit of thinking with an ownership spirit simply *refuses* to be swamped. When that person is given 24 things to do in a week, and he knows that he can only do seven, he is not *swamped* by that at all. He has a hundred words he can choose to use to respond to that situation, but he'll never choose "swamped" because he knows how fatiguing that would be.

He might even choose to be "amused" by the request. That would demonstrate a very high evolution of the spirit. At the very least, the owner can be "concerned" by the request and see an opportunity to have a very useful communication with the manager.

"I notice you have given me 24 things to do by the end of the week," the owner might say. "As you know, I am committed to doing a great job for you on everything I do. After looking at this list, I see that I probably can do seven of these things by the end of the week. I want to make sure that I do the seven things that you think are the most important, so I'm asking you to help prioritize them with me. If I finish the seven faster than I think I can, I'll certainly get to as many of the other 17 as I can. I'm not complaining or trying to get out of work, I just want to make sure I'm doing what you most want done."

If such a conversation is held in an optimistic spirit, with an absence of whining and martyrdom, then a genuine partnership can be formed between the owner and the manager.

Swamped by my own little kitten

Think of it in a different context: What if you got home at night and your little daughter came up to you and asked if you would do something for her? When you said yes, she pulled out a list and asked you to do 10 time-consuming things, including taking her to the mall, going to the zoo, playing in the backyard, and many more.

Would you feel hurt and offended and cry out, "Stop trying to *swamp* me!" or "You're swamping me!" Probably not. In fact, your most likely reaction would be amusement. "Whoa! Wait a minute, kitten," you would laugh. "We can't do all that tonight. I'm really happy you want to do that many things, but it's nighttime and I'm just home from work, so let's pick one thing together that we can do tonight and save the other things for later."

It wouldn't be a conversation filled with anger or resentment. So why does it have to be that way on the job?

Reinventing yourself involves processing out a lot of old, habitual language. It's not hard to do! People do it all the time. There is a lot of racially or sexually insensitive language that people have learned to drop altogether once they fully realize how offensive it is. This process is happening in society all the time.

So why can't it happen inside of you? There are words and phrases that offend the spirit. You don't have to believe them. Let them pass along.

30

The Saddest Story Ever Told

WHENEVER AN OWNER IS PRESENTED with a new adventure, a new game, or a new project, he or she uses such language as: "Count me in."

The owner will love trying something new and will say "count me in" with enthusiasm. The owner enjoys team spirit, and loves the game. Just as a child always wants to be taught how to play new games, the owner is up for just about anything new in life.

The victim, on the other hand, uses the words, "Wait and see"—about everything.

"How is that new job working out for you?" you might ask a victim.

"Oh, it's all right so far I suppose, but I'm going to wait and see. I've only been working there two years. I don't know how it's going to go."

You might see a victim you haven't seen for a number of years and say, "Hey, Bill, I heard you got married. Congratulations. How is that going for you?"

"Well, I don't know," says Bill. "We've only been married a year now, so I don't really know. We'll wait and see. I'm kind of waiting for the other shoe to drop."

The victim is usually uncomfortable if things are going well in life, and is not afraid to tell you so.

"Things are going great for me right now," says the victim, "and that's what bothers me. When things are going well like this I'm always nervous, because I know something big is about to happen; something awful is coming around the bend. You know it's true that there's always a calm before the storm. And because I don't know for sure what's coming, I'm having a hard time sleeping these days."

The loss of sleep causes the victim to become accident-prone and not alert to details. Soon, big mistakes *are* made and accidents start to happen. The other shoe sure does fall. A victim's thoughts are a self-fulfilling prophecy.

Victims don't trust the good times and almost welcome the bad news. Their story about life is so deeply habituated to be pessimistic that they experience discomfort when they step outside their story. Victims, for example, have a hard time being praised and acknowledged. It goes against their story. Their story says that they don't get any respect.

Victims are like the late comedian Rodney Dangerfield. His comedic bit was that he never got any respect anywhere he went, when he would say that he went to his physician he was told he was overweight and needed to lose a lot of pounds. He said to the doctor, "I'd like to get a second opinion," and the doctor replied, "Okay, you're ugly, too."

Victims have built their wholes live around their stories of disrespect. They aren't aware that our stories are self-created. You can begin a new story about yourself today.

First, look for opportunities to say, "Count me in," and "Hey, I'll play!" Look for a chance to make a fool of yourself. Don't be afraid to lose face and fail at something. Don't reject the idea of coming across as a human being. Jump in. Play. Fall down. Get up. Play harder. Come home with a dirty face and sweat on your neck. Take a bath. And sleep.

You lived life that way when you were young, and you can do it again. You can sleep again.

31

Why Don't You Feel Offended?

AN INTERESTING ILLUSTRATION OF THE owner-victim distinction occurred awhile back as I was watching Matt Lauer of the *Today Show* attempt to make Tiger Woods's father admit he was offended by some public remarks made by one Fuzzy Zoeller.

Fuzzy Zoeller is a professional golfer. He had made some sarcastic racist remarks in the midst of his bitterness at having been beaten in a tournament so badly by the young black superstar Tiger Woods.

But on the *Today Show,* Tiger's father refused to be a victim of any of this. Matt Lauer repeatedly urged him to say how offended he was by Fuzzy's remarks, and he said he *wasn't offended.* He said the remarks were Zoeller's problem, not his. The remarks didn't bother him in the slightest.

"But sir, he offended your culture," said Lauer.

"No, he didn't. The culture's fine. Fuzzy Zoeller's got the problem. We don't."

Victim-seekers in the media usually feel a little betrayed when their ongoing treasure hunt for victim guests gets frustrated by a real owner. They become uncomfortable when they can't talk someone into being a victim of something. You could see a slight sheen of sweaty panic cover Matt Lauer's face as the elder and elegant Mr. Woods refused to be victimized.

It was a rare and satisfying moment of television viewing. We always enjoy it when someone refuses to play victim. Like Eleanor Roosevelt, for example. "No one can make me feel inferior," she said, "without my permission."

One of the victim's signature words is "offended." Victims are offended easily and often during the course of the day.

They can be offended in a number of ways. They can be offended by something that is said on the radio coming into work. They can be offended by an e-mail from management. They can be offended by something someone said at lunch. And they can be offended by a decision made by a spouse.

I know the habit of feeling offended and how it wears me down. To be offended is to surrender to the brute power of other people. It is to give people permission all day to make me feel resentful. I don't even realize that every time I speak the words, "That offends me," I am committing an attack on my own spirit.

An owner of the spirit has a different habit when it comes to this situation. The owner says: *"You can't offend me."*

Even when someone apologizes to the owner for offending him or her, the owner refuses to play along.

"You didn't offend me," the owner will say, "because you can't offend me. I don't give that to you."

"Oh come on now," says the apologist. "I'm certain I offended you this morning, and I'm just here to offer my apology. I also want to apologize for the racial remark I made."

"It didn't offend me," says the owner.

"Not even the racial slur?"

"Nope."

Seeing that the person is still not satisfied, the owner might want to add something.

"You really didn't offend me, because you can't offend me. I simply don't give that to you. However, I will say this: You are *offensive*. And as for that racial remark, I had you written up. But please try to see that this is about you, not me. I'm just fine."

My friend Jerry Traylor once made a long-distance run across the United States, from California to New York. This seemed like a logical adventure to Jerry who had run a number of marathons, climbed Pike's Peak, and jumped out of an airplane. That Jerry was born with cerebral palsy just made things more interesting to him.

But to the media, it gave them what they wanted, a headline. When Jerry completed his run across the country, the headline in *USA Today* said, "Palsy Victim Runs Across the USA."

"Victim?" asked Jerry as he held up the newspaper's headline to a group of people he and I were meeting with. "How about victor?"

Break that offensive habit

Notice your feelings the next time you tell yourself that you are offended. See if you can turn your thinking around. It takes a little practice, but I promise you can do it. Put the responsibility back on the person who has been offensive. Stand strong in the face of offensive behavior and refuse to be a victim of it. Refuse to have it make you a martyr and someone to be pitied. Turn it back on the person who generated it so *they* can take it on, not you. You can then invent a self that finds it easy to say, "No one can offend me."

What would you rather do? Would you rather go to the offensive person a week later and say, "Because of what you said I have been crying softly into my pillow every night for a week."?

Reinventing yourself always goes toward your independence and birthright of power. That's why reinventing yourself is so satisfying a project to take on. It makes its own pursuit more and more fun.

32

Saying No to the Boys on the Side

My youngest sister, Cindy, is as much of an owner of the spirit as anyone I know.

In *100 Ways to Motivate Yourself,* I wrote about her and how her childhood hero was Amelia Earhart, and how Cindy studied the great aviator's life and got inspired enough to take flying lessons and solo in a small plane.

"I've never been that scared ever before," Cindy said. "Being up there alone in that plane, my mouth went completely dry."

Cindy has reinvented herself repeatedly in life. Gently and creatively. Always toward the spirit. Her "personality" is never the same from one year to the next because she's always adding something.

After taking flying lessons, she attended a theological college in Denver, Colorado. Yet another reinvention.

Throughout her growth, one thing has remained constant: her respect for her commitments. I have learned a lot from her on that score. For example, I'll never forget my disbelief when Cindy once turned down an opportunity to play a significant part in a big scene in a motion picture. It took more ownership on her part than I could even imagine having at the time.

Whoopi Goldberg was in Tucson, Arizona, filming *Boys on the Side* when Cindy was encouraged to answer a casting call for local extras for the movie. Cindy, who owned a T-shirt company at the time, decided to do it, just for the fun of it.

After a short interview and a photo session, Cindy went back to her business, expecting nothing. But they called right away and told her that they wanted her for two things: as a stand-in for one of the Indigo Girls, and for a part in a scene that would depict Whoopi's character's birthday party. Cindy said she was delighted and asked how long they wanted her. She was told "one full day's shoot. That's all."

Cindy went to the movie set, and stayed the entire day, working on the scene and thoroughly enjoying the experience of being in a major Hollywood movie.

But it was Whoopi's birthday party

The next day, she returned to her T-shirt business, which had fallen a little behind the day she was away. When she got to work, her employees were all excited. They said the movie set had called and the director needed Cindy to return right away for more shooting.

Cindy said no.

She said the agreement was for one day, and her commitment to her customers and the orders would take priority. She thanked them for asking.

When I heard about this I flipped out.

"You told them whaaaat?!" I shouted to Cindy over the phone. "You told them *no*??? Whoopi Goldberg. *The* Whoopi Goldberg. You turned down a chance for more shooting, an expanded part? What were you thinking??"

"I was thinking that I needed to take care of business and that I had already kept my agreement and kept my word with the director when I told him I would give him the one full day that he had requested." Cindy was very calm. "It isn't just T-shirts to me," she said. "It's a matter of keeping my word with my customers. How could a movie be more important than that?"

"Did they get mad at you? Were they upset?"

"Oh yes!" she started laughing. "They really went bananas. The director called and called and told me I couldn't do that to him. It was really bizarre after a while because he kept saying things like, '*But it's Whoopi's birthday. You're supposed to be at Whoopi's birthday.*' I told him, 'Now sir, you and I both know it's not Whoopi's birthday. It's a movie. You know it's a movie and I know it's a movie. So please, let me run my business.'"

To an owner, a commitment is everything.

Your commitments are creations

An owner's self-talk around her relationship to commitments is powerful and simple: "I create the commitments in my life. They are mine. I can create them or destroy them."

A victim has no such relationship to a commitment. To a victim, commitments are simply feelings. They come and go, like stomach gas.

"I'm not feeling the same commitment to my wife as I used to," victims will say. "I don't feel as committed to this job as I once did."

But commitments are not feelings. They are gentle internal decisions. And it's only by seeing that all our commitments have been decisions, that we can honor those decisions. We can refresh them each day. A commitment can become a part of our life that we are peaceful about.

Reinvention occurs, not in overworked frenzy, but in peace. In the most peaceful center of our being. A silent, gentle decision is made, and a new you is created.

When you change your relationship to commitments so that they are now quiet decisions inside of you, you won't have to revisit them. You just check in with them every morning to remember what they are.

33

A Kite Rises Against the Wind

ONCE YOU BEGIN REINVENTING YOURSELF, you'll soon find all kinds of way to become inspired.

There is no energy surge like the surge of pure inspiration. It's a state of mind that novelist Vladimir Nabokov was talking about when he said, "You experience a shuddering sensation of wild magic, of some inner resurrection, as if a dead man were revived by a sparkling drug that has been rapidly mixed in your presence."

A victim, on the other hand, feels the opposite of inspired. A victim feels discouraged. This discouragement arises naturally from the language the victim uses to think about life.

"Life is unfair," the victim observes. "I don't use life, life uses *me*." The victim thinks, "I didn't ask to be born. No one consulted me about it."

When something negative or disappointing happens to the victim, the victim explains it with, "That's life!" "That's life: Riding high in April, shot down in May."

The word "life" is almost always used to explain the most tragic and disappointing things. After thinking and talking about life for a while, the victim becomes tired and discouraged. It's a subject that gets him down.

A victim might come to work on Monday with his arm in a sling. If you ask what happened, he might say, "Oh, I was trying to fix the air conditioner on my roof and I fell. But . . . *that's life*. If it's not one thing, it's something else. Isn't that the truth? Life's just one damned thing after another!"

It is! But only because you *say* it is.

Because a victim uses an internal language that reflects a futile attempt to please other people, a victim almost always ends up resenting other people. The victim then tries to get even with the people he resents by talking behind their backs. No one enjoys living a life of living up to other people's expectations.

"We gossip about others," said Krishnamurti, "because we are not sufficiently interested in the process of our own thinking and our own action."

The owner, on the other hand, doesn't obsess about other people's opinions. The owner does not fear other people. Therefore, *the owner is more free to enjoy other people.*

Even when the owner is in the presence of a maladjusted victim who is trying to lord it over the owner, the owner does not get offended. The owner does not base his life on what the victim thinks.

The owner sees everyone as a kind of teacher. Every experience has the potential to be, if thought about long enough, a learning experience: "Even pessimistic people have something to teach me. Even nasty experiences have something inside them I can learn from."

In her powerful song "You Learn," Alanis Morisette captures the owner's spirit when she sings:

> You grieve, you learn.
> You choke, you learn.
> You laugh, you learn.
> You choose, you learn.
> You pray, you learn.
> You ask, you learn.
> You live, you learn.

But victims never seem to learn. They are always asking, in the face of a setback, "Why does this always happen to me?"

That's why victims get their feelings hurt a lot. It's because they are living on such a low level of mental energy that their reactions to other people are simply emotional rather than thoughtful. Victims take other people personally, so they are easily wounded. It's a negative feedback loop that pulls them down their emotional ladder with each negative thought.

Owners, on the other hand, can actually use the disrespect of another person as a challenge that may ultimately lift them even higher. An owner, like a kite, rises *against* the wind. Consider these words from Michael Jordan as he talked about his final years in the NBA:

> Challenge me. Doubt me. Disrespect me. Tell me I'm older. Tell me I can no longer fly. I want you to.

You can invent yourself to be someone who thinks of everything that happens in life as a teaching moment—a treasured source of challenge. You can use variations of the thoughts, "I use life," and "Life is pure opportunity."

You'll wake up in the morning and immediately welcome the breath of life. (Remember: The original meaning of the word "spirit" is "breath.")

Grateful for another day, you will learn to see this day as a whole life in microcosm. "I am born with the sun in the morning and I will die to the day as I fall asleep tonight." You'll be happy to follow philosopher Seneca, who said, "Count each day a separate life." Or philosopher-coach John Wooden, who said, "Make each day your masterpiece."

Part Four

Setting Your "Self" on Fire

We possess such immense resources
of power that pessimism is a laughable absurdity.
—Colin Wilson

34

Now You Can Ride With No Hands

You really can reinvent yourself. You did it constantly when you were little, and you can do it again now.

All your life you've been told, "Just be yourself!" But that's the worst thing you could have done. It was other fearful people trying to enroll you in the worldwide human conspiracy of frozen personality.

As a child, you knew in your soul that you didn't know *how* to "be yourself." You knew the advice made no sense. Because there was no single self to be! There were many "yous," and you invented new ones all the time—for the fun of it, because as a child you had energy. When you were born, you entered this world "trailing clouds of glory." You were connected to your spirit, and you knew that happiness came from taking effective action upon the universe. That was your fun.

You shouted out with joy as you ran across the playground to meet a friend. You went to the beach and played happily in the freezing ocean waves. You dug deep in the wet sand and made a castle. You saved a baby bird's life. You made costumes at night and you were anyone you wanted to be, any time you wanted.

You were Snow White. You were Superman. You flew across your room into dreams of your own making. You got up in the morning and got on your bike. The whole world was sleeping. You rode with no hands.

And you can do it again.

Perhaps you're thinking that now that you've grown up, you no longer know what to do with your life. But you can start something anyway. *Doing it* will tell you what it should be. You can only see it on the wing.

I know how your parents treated you, I remember the mental pictures you painted. Your parents aren't the problem. You are. If your personality can kidnap your current happiness, you are the problem.

And that's good news, because if you're the problem, you're also the solution. So set yourself on fire, by setting your "self" on fire.

I write today only to breathe my life into yours. That's what the word *inspire* really means. It means if I can do this, you can, too. Because I have failed so many times, I succeed. Losing is not the same as being defeated.

Just trust these facts: People change. People become happy. Happiness becomes a thing to be mastered.

I will always refuse to buy into your fear that you won't be able to fly. You *can* fly. It is a mathematical law that we can love anyone we want, and all of life is mathematical.

Any sadness you're feeling now is only your fatigue. The problem is that it just feels like home, feels familiar and safe. This sadness only teaches you how to live in the past. It's a negative feedback loop that curls around your ankle and pulls you down your ladder of selves. The paradox is this: Fatigue is caused by feeling fatigued. Weariness comes from quitting. (A paradox is not a contradiction. When you see it, it is a joy forever.)

Thomas Jefferson saw the other side of the same paradox. When he had his paradoxical enlightenment, he exclaimed, "The more you do, the more you *can* do!"

Is it cold in here? Or is it you? If you're cold, you can take some of this light, and you can let it shine. Let it shine through the magnifying glass of your mind and start a fire that burns all your old selves to the ground, all the sophisticated characters you used to play.

You can dance, like distance runners do, across the earth. You already know you can do it.

Because, anything I can do, you can do better. Someone from a far off seaside land said the very same thing once, but very few people ever believed it.

But you don't even have to believe it to get it started. It's a gentle and easy thing to start.

Here's how to start: Rather than asking yourself what you *feel like* doing, ask yourself: "What needs to be done?" Believe it or not, your joyful reinvention will begin by doing what's necessary, by being in action. The reason people aren't *busy being born* into the person they would really like to be is because they are not busy, period. They are wasting all their time wondering if they *feel* right, wondering what their emotions are trying to tell them, and wondering why they are not happy.

Happiness comes to those who are busy *doing*. Happiness follows in the slipstream of the actions you take. It's not something you have to feel first.

All you have to do is wake up and ask yourself what kind of future you would like to create, and then ask the most important question you'll ever ask yourself: "What needs to be done?"

You will *know* what needs to be done. It's never a mystery. Your invented future is waiting for you. All it asks is for you to get busy. Do what needs to be done. That's a necessity. And necessity, as you knew it all along, is the mother of invention. Not dreams or feelings or self-respect or confidence or trust or love or any of that. Just the doing of what needs to be done. Do it badly; do it slowly; do it fearfully; do it any way you have to, but do it.

35

How Much Ego Do You Need to Succeed?

MOST PEOPLE I WORK WITH believe that reinventing yourself requires a major building up of the ego. You must learn to take care of Number One. You have to overcome your humble, introverted nature and burst upon the world with real swagger.

My experience has been the opposite.

My experience has been that the bigger the ego someone has, the harder it is for them to learn new ways of being. Learning becomes a threat to who they think they already are.

Another consequence of an inflated ego is that it makes it hard for people to relax in the presence of such a force. It can be intimidating and a source of great agitation to be in the presence of a large and serious ego. Hard to connect. Hard to trust.

Yet a lot of personal development teaching leads people in this direction. It tries to help people enlarge their egos so that they can assert themselves more aggressively in a very competitive world.

The best reinventions I've seen and been a part of are by people who do not build the ego up. They actually trim it down. It becomes an act of creative deconstruction. Subtraction rather than addition. A carving away of the fixed personality, like a sculptor carves the clay away.

What are the negative, heavy, judgmental beliefs you have about yourself? Let's start pruning those away. What are you believing about your permanent personality? Let's start letting that drop away, too. Let's open you up. Because when your ego drops away, you don't get smaller (as we all initially fear we would) you actually expand. You open up to all kinds of opportunities and possibilities you never knew were there.

When you start questioning what you believe about yourself all those limitations that you think you have start to fall away. If you go all the way with this when I ask you who you are you might even say, "I'm wide open!" All those fears you thought you needed to cling to to keep you "safe" no longer apply. That's called reinventing yourself.

The less you believe about yourself, the more open you are to intuition coming through you. Intuition needs open space to come through. It gets blocked by fixed personalities trying to cling to clusters of beliefs.

On the other hand, the more you try to build up your ego, the harder it is to listen to others. Your mind is too occupied with maintenance of an image. A personal brand you are holding onto for dear life. A large ego is always trying to make an impression. And that drives people away.

I noticed right off that my own coach, Steve Hardison, had no feeling of superiority to anyone. His humility was his power. He was as happy to be talking to a homeless person as he was to a billionaire entrepreneur. He always said he was not "better" than anyone even though he knew he had enormous power as a coach. When asked how his masterful coaching worked, he would say, "You talk and I listen and then I talk and you listen." Very simple.

Another thing he taught me was that the world was a stage and we could play any part we wanted once we got over ourselves. Whenever I faced a challenge, or a thing I didn't think I could do, he would ask me, "Who would you need to be?" to do that thing. Soon, after years of working with him, I saw that such a choice was always wide open, and that a happy, successful life was one of continuous, spontaneous reinvention.

Later in my life, as I was taking on clients of my own I found that anyone could do that. Anyone could reinvent on the spot. And the alternative was staying stuck forever. Whenever people saw that alternative, they became very interested in learning to reinvent.

Do you need a life coach or should you just wing it?

A lot of people who know I do life coaching ask me, "Do I need a life coach? How would I know?"

No one needs a life coach. It isn't a matter of need. It's a matter of want. The relationship has to be generated from your own desire.

It's not therapy, just as this book is not therapy. It's about creativity. I sometimes like to over-simplify it by saying that therapy is to heal your past and coaching is to create your future. Coaching is not medicinal. It comes from the world of sports and from the arts. There are voice coaches, dialect coaches, hitting coaches, and life coaches.

When I got a coach for myself I had already done a lot of therapy. I was ready to leave the past behind, like the dead leaves in autumn. Colorful, yes, but completely dead and gone. I wanted to create the future. I wanted to reinvent myself. Coaching was the ticket for me.

But you can do it any way you want. Books. Retreats. Online seminars. The methods are many. The desire is all that is needed. That and a willingness to see that invention is all we were born to do. Why not turn our innate creativity (something everybody has) toward our own lives, so that our future and our made-up "self" can be a work of art?

36

The Hidden Downside of Winning Friends and Influencing People

I SPENT A LARGE PART of my early professional life trying to win friends and influence people. I had heard that that was how to succeed. I never saw the flaw in that approach.

Finally I saw it. My attempts to win people over and influence them had me subconsciously thinking of other people as different. It was almost as if I regarded them as alien beings from another planet. How do I learn their ways? How do I win them over?

It's what I would ask if I landed on another planet.

It was an approach to professional life that emphasized pleasing instead of serving. It tempted me into flattery and manipulation. It made compassion hard to feel, and it actually

177

created distance between me and other people. Other people had become mere targets of opportunity. Targets instead of real people. Like in a military game.

But I started to notice that truly successful companies and people didn't treat people that way. They were kind, compassionate and giving. They went right to the heart of people. They called it profound service, and it led to business success and personal fulfillment.

I became a convert. Instead of asking myself, "How can I win this person's admiration?" I started asking, "How can I serve this person?" and "How might I contribute to this person's life right now?"

It was a reinvention of attention. It took me away from my perceived needs and had me more focused on theirs. And far from feeling like a sacrificial doormat, the sense of fun and fulfillment grew (as did my prosperity and client list). It was a way of getting over myself so that I could get into the client's world and out of my own. A much more adventurous life! Traveling to other worlds all day instead of hiding out in my own.

• • •

My client Rebecca called me because she was worried about a chamber of commerce mixer she was going to attend. Rebecca was a business consultant who wasn't comfortable in social situations even though she thought it would help her business to get out into the world and meet people.

"How do I present myself?" she asked. "How do I explain what I do? I'm really not good at this."

We decided to work on a different approach. I asked her to imagine that this event was not about her. That it wouldn't matter if she was invisible if she approached it from the standpoint of pure curiosity. What if it was about the other people?

Rebecca caught on fast and said maybe she would show up as Jessica Fletcher (her favorite TV detective) and simply ask a lot of gentle questions as she met people. She wouldn't have to prepare any form of self-promotion, or way of being, but could simply be curiosity itself.

Later she told me she loved the event. She loved being a detective. It was a perfect reinvention for her. People connected with her and enjoyed her attention and high levels of interest in their lives and work. Many relationships grew out of this event for Rebecca because people felt such a connection to her.

Many people think they have to be a consistent foghorn of personal confidence, self-promotion and non-stop verbal branding. They miss the potential for reinvention into becoming a profoundly creative listener.

37

Your Career Played as a Game, Versus Your Career as a Grind for Survival

ONE REASON I STAYED STUCK for so long in a personality that was not succeeding was that I thought that personality was fixed. I also thought that personality was responsible for all my troubles. How do you reinvent a fixed personality?

I decided to try not taking it all so seriously.

That's when true reinvention happened for me. Because I got very lucky in discovering a life coach and business coach (Steve Hardison) who saw through the illusion of personal permanence, I began to play my business as a game. Instead of seeing it as a life-or-death struggle for survival.

I stopped fearing "rejection." When people not chose not to use my services I saw it as mere information. I began to play with people and not be intimidated by them. And after a few years of ever-increasing success I started coaching clients to do the same—to stop taking themselves so seriously and start adding in a game element to all they were doing. Soon their own results were improving, too.

We often grow up believing truisms that aren't even true. Such as "getting serious" about doing something will make you more likely to do it. Not really true!

Our parents and teachers and guardians would tell us it was time to "get serious" and stop slacking off. So we grew up believing that was the way to start accomplishing things. And later in life we kept trying to motivate ourselves that way. Get serious!

I would keep telling myself it was time to get serious about my studies. And then I would go to a party instead. I didn't see the hidden dynamic at play: The more serious my thoughts became, the heavier I felt and the colder it felt inside. From that heavy, cold place I lost all inspiration to be productive or do something great.

Ralph Waldo Emerson is famous for saying that "nothing great was ever created without enthusiasm." That looks true! And yet enthusiasm is linked with fun. Not with heaviness or seriousness.

Turning a formerly weighty task into a game releases new energy and creativity, and improves the volume and quality of our work.

One reason people initially resist this life-changing insight is that they associate game playing with trivial and frivolous activity. But my experience (and that of an increasing number of my clients) shows that games are almost always played with bright devotion and focus. One of the reasons so many people love to watch sports is how exciting it is to see people perform with such a high level of wit and enthusiasm.

● ● ●

Marcus was a salesperson who dreaded his work day and feared failure. He was taking his life very seriously. After we had a few conversations in which he finally saw how heavy his thoughts had become, he was finally open to doing things differently.

As he looked back on his past experience of life he saw how he was a much more alive and creative person when he was playing his favorite interactive multiple-player computer game than he was out there in "the real world." He saw the profound difference between game-playing Marcus and working Marcus. So he was open to reinventing working Marcus.

As he made his sales communications throughout the day he started keeping score. He put his sales calls on a big scoreboard in his office and he began competing with who he was the previous week. He then enlisted the participation of another salesperson on his team for some friendly competition. He started tracking all kinds of activities and going for a "personal best" any time he could. As he started seeing improved results in his commission income the games became even more fun. It inspired him to start reading books by top sales authors so he could increase his skills and put up even better numbers. Work had become play. It was no longer a grind.

"I'm having serious fun," he texted me recently when I asked how he was doing. He was now in charge of a division of sales people and he enjoyed coaching them on lightening up and learning to enjoy the game of business. In their meeting room there were scoreboards, standings, photos celebrating winners of contests, and an atmosphere of happy play. Amazing the numbers you can put up when you are not taking work life so seriously.

38

Does Success Make You Happy or Does Happiness Make You Successful?

I USED TO DO A lot of sales training. I'd work with sales teams, giving them seminars and workshops about sales psychology, communication techniques, time management, etc.

In the course of this work I noticed something fascinating. I noticed that happiness was a predictor of sales success. The happiest people on the team were the ones who were selling the most.

Many of my colleagues scoffed at that discovery. They said that of course successful sales people are happy, you'd be happy too if you were succeeding at making those big commissions.

But they had it backward.

The more I talked to sales managers and CEOs about their top performers the more I learned that these people were extremely happy even when they arrived. Even when they were struggling, they maintained an optimistic, cheerful out-look. People enjoyed being around them. Happiness can be contagious.

Later I learned that what I was observing on the sales teams I was training has been studied, researched, and well-documented by psychologists in the emerging field of Positive Psychology. I started studying the books of pioneers in that field, like Martin Seligman and Barbara Fredrickson to con-firm what I was seeing. And one of the most encouraging findings made by Dr. Seligman (captured in his book *Learned Optimism*) was that optimism could be learned. We can spend a whole life as a pessimist and with the right learning and encouragement become a total optimist.

Once again life was showing me that reinventing myself was not a pipe dream or some naïve new age quest. It was a real and true possibility for anyone and everyone.

39

What to Do About My Money Fears?

MOST OF MY LIFE I had so many fears about money (and my continuous lack thereof) that the thought of reinventing myself never had a chance to take hold.

But once I saw that creating wealth came from delivering profound, creative service to others, everything changed. I was able to drop the old stories I had around money, and how my past history had left me incapable of being a prosperous, responsible adult. I stopped focusing on who I thought I was and what I thought my shortcomings were, and I began focusing on others, and how I could serve them.

My days, previously, had been days filled with failed sales calls. I thought I had to learn how to deal with rejection because there was so much of it! I was taking everything personally. I was taking money personally. I was always wondering if I was *worthy* of becoming successful and prosperous.

But the world shifted when I replaced the word *worthy* with the word **useful**. As a potential client interacted with me

I started asking myself how I might be useful to that person or that company. I took the focus off of me and put it on them. I got into their world and started helping them solve their problems. Soon they were bringing me back in with larger contracts and better fees. The less I focused on myself, the faster my money problems became a thing of the past.

I began to realize that reinventing myself was happening, but in a strange and unexpected way. I wasn't changing from one kind of person to another. I was leaving the whole permanent person thing behind and replacing it with action. I was replacing it with listening, compassion, curiosity and more action.

As I saw that money fears disappeared at the same rate that I myself disappeared, it became fun. I could show up to my work life empty, the same way a paramedic shows up to an accident scene empty, not knowing what (s)he's going to do until (s)he gets there—not worried about personality, past history, or anything permanent like that.

People said I was changing. People thought I'd reinvented myself. And to outward appearances, I had. I was no longer anything like the fearful, broke person I used to be. But what was hard to explain was that this new "self" was no self at all. No permanent thing. Just action. Just service livened up by fun and freewheeling activity.

40

Engineering Dreams Into Reality

MOST OF MY LIFE, I have hated motivational speakers. In fact, when my old friends hear that I have *become* a motivational speaker, they are shocked.

Of course, we all know that no one can be motivated by another person. Not in the long run. Motivation has to come from within, or else it's worth nothing.

That's why I disliked motivational speakers so much: because they wouldn't motivate me, they would only temporarily stimulate me. They would stimulate me emotionally with stories about athletes who overcame handicaps. And just when they got me hooked into their feelings of hope, they would leave my life forever and, try as I might, I could never get the feeling back.

Instead of giving me something to *use*, they gave me a big, noisy emotional high, and the sense that "*that* was a great speaker!"

To me, motivational speakers were like secular evangelists prancing across the stage, their voices soaring with drama as they told stories about people they had never met doing heroic things that *they themselves would never dream of doing*. Most of them sounded like they memorized their third-hand stories from old copies of *Reader's Digest*. To see these "motivators" in person was not a pleasant experience. Most dressed like morticians and flew across the stage like they had just shot up methamphetamines before being introduced.

Enter a master of the mind

One day I met a different kind of motivator. His entire focus was human thought, not sentimental emotion. His commitment was to teach the inner workings of the mind so that people could, in his words, "master" their minds forever. He had founded a company dedicated to that end, and he had called it the Mind Masters Institute.

At first, I laughed cynically when I heard the name.

"What do you do?" I asked. "Teach people how to bend spoons with their thoughts?"

But he wasn't deterred by my cynicism. He smiled and patiently explained that the mind could be mastered, and we humans, once doing this, could do whatever we wanted to. He was serious. He didn't rant and rave about attitude and compassion and emotions, he taught about thinking. While everyone else in the world was telling us *what* to think, this person was telling us *how* to think.

His name is Dennis Deaton. The first time I heard him speak, it was to a group of car salespeople who were having a bad sales month. I was doing the dealership's advertising at the time, and the sales manager asked me to hire a motivational speaker for a midmonth breakfast they were having for all employees to try to rally the sagging sales figures.

I had no idea who to hire because I hated motivational speakers. Finally, a friend of mine recommended Dr. Deaton, so I hired him without ever having heard him and not expecting much of anything.

What I heard when Deaton spoke was completely different than what I was used to. He was only interested in one thing: the interplay between the mind and the brain. He spoke with passion about his subject, but not to artificially pump the crowd up. He spoke so that they would become excited about *knowing something* about how their biocomputers worked. He spoke with a commitment to be *useful* rather than just entertaining.

Not only did the salespeople go out and have their biggest sales month that year after Deaton's speech, but I felt my entire life change from it. I made a vow after he had left the building that someday I would be working with him. I wanted to join him in the work he was doing, teaching about the mind. I somehow knew that if I forced myself to know how to teach it, I myself could learn it.

Because I failed so often, I succeed

One of the things that made my eventual partnering with Deaton so interesting was how different he and I were from each other. He had succeeded throughout his life, at sports, in academics, you name it.

I, on the other hand, had not. But despite our different results with success, Deaton and I took an immediate liking to each other, and he taught me everything he knew. He was completely unselfish about my teaching his work. His trade-marked "Visioneering" process for "engineering goals into reality" was something I began immediately to apply to my own life.

Because it was based on the workings of the brain, it worked. There was no emotional pump in it. It was a cold-blooded course in how to get your mind and brain to interact in such a way that your visions for your own future become reality. It was clear and it was effective.

Using Deaton's system, I started setting and achieving goals at an unusually fast pace. My whole life turned around. Instead of using my brain all day to picture what I feared, he had taught me to use it to picture what I wanted.

My audiences, too, were connecting with me. When I spoke of my former life, they could see the truth in the misery of it. Most of them could identify. It wasn't hard for them to verify what a losing proposition I had been. If visioneering could work for me, they realized, it could work for anyone.

Soon it was becoming fun for people to take some of the seminars from a lifelong winner such as Dennis, and then hear the perspective of a late bloomer such as myself. Many people who might have been skeptical about our principles really working would hear my life stories and think, "Well, if he can do it, I can. I was never *that* bad."

You are not as low as I was

I was a truly confused non-achiever. I won't go into all of it, but I was. Take my word for it. I still sometimes notice that the wreckage of my past floats ashore for me to clean up. It's a grim but good reminder. As I pick up the pieces of the shattered

Titanic that was me, I am reminded of how easy it was to live at so low and confused a level.

You cannot tell me anything about yourself that would surprise me. You cannot offend me. You cannot shock me. You couldn't be focusing on this book if you were as low as I once was. You couldn't be holding it in your hands or comprehending it. Reading this, you're already ahead of where I was.

In fact, the lower you are now, the more fun you are going to have if you take reinvention on as a personal project. Every word in this book is part of my overall goal to get you to understand that you can make yourself up as you go along. You can redesign yourself completely, and not because there's necessarily anything *wrong* with you, but just for the sheer joy of reinvention. There is no joy like it.

In fact, when I began to really achieve things, it was after dropping the idea that there was anything really wrong with me.

The way I got started back to the spirit was this: I began to allow myself to think in a relaxed and clear way. It sounds almost too simple, but I found that true victims don't do it. They don't relax. They brood and ruminate and worry. And then they feel depressed. And then they feel angry. And then they feel self-pity. And the deadly beat goes on. The negative cycle circles back on itself.

A woman in a workshop once told me, "Self-pity is like a worm that gets in your brain and lays its eggs there."

Here's what I finally allowed myself to think: What if it were true that *I become what I think about* all day long? What would I want to think about? If I knew I would become what that was, what would I want it to be?

That was the first step on my way out. It can be your first step, too, no matter where you are.

Plato kept saying it, but we would not listen: "Thinking is the soul talking to itself."

Victims will not want this to be true. They will want to cite examples, such as Vincent van Gogh, and say that he was too beautiful to live in this cruel world. But it was the opposite. The *world* was too beautiful for a victim like him to accept, except in his paintings.

His personal life was all victim. He had invented such a convincing victim personality that the beauty and truth that showed up in a painting such as *Starry Night* drove him crazy. It was too big a contradiction.

He knew his depression was a creation just as his paintings were, but he didn't know what to do about it. He could paint it, but he couldn't think it. In the end, his depressing self-portrait won out.

For me to save my own soul, I had to let it begin talking to itself. I had to let it split in two: witness and thinker. I began to watch what happened to my life when I became more practiced at witnessing my own thinking.

"Your mind is an instrument, a tool," said Eckhart Tolle. "It is there to be used for a specific task, and when the task is completed, you lay it down. As it is, I would say about 80 to 90 percent of most people's thinking is not only repetitive and useless, but because of its dysfunctional and often negative nature, much of it is also harmful. Observe your mind and you will find this to be true. It causes a serious leakage of vital energy."

My witnessing observer inside feels like the human spirit, and in normal times it remains quiet while old voices from the past take its place in my brain. The old voices belong to my teachers, peers, siblings, and parents, their shaming and condemnation echoing throughout my skull telling me they are the voice of my own conscience! Without stepping back to see the nature of that faulty thinking, I take those critical voices to be my own.

"You should do it!" one voice says. "You're obligated to do it! Stop being so selfish! Any kind of organized person would have done it by now!" And then I end up not doing it, because a voice of shame and judgment is not a very inspiring voice. It's an annoying voice.

But inside all of us, there is a deeper, stronger voice that eventually starts to talk back. It says, "Don't tell me what to do." We somehow love that voice. It is the voice of the rebel in us, the part that does not care about other people's judgments. It is the greatest part of who we are. And we want to learn to increase the volume on that voice, because the clearer it gets, the freer we become.

The volume of the negative voices from the past can be turned down a little more each day until the voice of the real you, the voice of the spirit, emerges to rule your life and lead you in the pursuit of reinvention and happiness. Reinvention merely means growth. And we are happy when we are growing.

41

Your Happiness Is Not Selfish

THE VOICE OF STRENGTH IN a crisis is also the voice that can lead you in your journey to happiness, once you see the value of that journey. Once you see the value of happiness.

A lot of us have been confused abut the pursuit of happiness. It seems we have been yelled at so many times about being "selfish" that we have equated our own happiness with incorrect behavior. But cultivating and strengthening our own happiness is not selfish. Especially because of how much it benefits others.

For example, one of the best gifts a parent can give a child is to be a happy parent. One of the best gifts a wife can give to a husband is her own personal happiness. Her joy in living is one of the most gratifying things he experiences. If she relates to him in a depressed, testy, needy, emotional way, it becomes tough to live with. She is hardly a gift to him, and vice versa.

Much of the "pain of love" expressed in our great popular music is really the pain of unfulfilled neediness. When singers sing, "Love hurts...," they don't really mean love. They should be singing, "Dependency hurts . . ." (except they probably wouldn't have a hit song).

In her brilliant novel of ownership and personal creativity, *Atlas Shrugged,* Ayn Rand makes the best case ever made up to that point about the power of personal happiness, and the damage done to us by unhappy people who have become sanctimonious do-gooders. This is the passage from that novel cited recently by Nathaniel Branden in his psychological masterpiece, *The Art of Consciousness:*

> Why is it moral to serve the happiness of others and not your own? If enjoyment is a value, why is it moral when experienced by others, but immoral when experienced by you? Why is it immoral for you to desire, but moral for others to do so? Why is it immoral to produce a value and keep it, but moral to give it away? And if it is not moral for you to keep a value, why is it moral for others to accept it? If you are selfless and virtuous when you give it, are they not selfish and vicious when they take it? Does virtue consist of serving vice?

Happy people have more to give others. They have more energy and they have more life. A happy person owns a spirit that adds power to any act of giving.

A person who is angry and depressed and "serving" someone out of a sense of obligation is poisoning the "gift" with resentment. Such giving is not really giving. It is a form of acting out a feeling of obligation. It is trying to live up to someone else's expectation. It is the daily life of a victim.

Such victims are passive observers of their own mental fatigue and sadness. They think there's nothing they can do about it. They don't understand that there's another part of the brain *just waiting* to be activated, another voice just waiting to have the light turned on. It's the voice of the human spirit.

All reinvention involves nurturing that primal voice of freedom. Reinventing yourself is not a matter of going from bad to good, but rather from victim to owner. Take charge of your happiness. It's a creation, so start building it.

42

And You Shall Have the Power

A YOUNG NOVELIST FOUND MY e-mail address through a friend and wrote to me about his problems motivating himself. He had been reading *100 Ways to Motivate Yourself,* but he had to confess that he was currently stuck.

"I lose faith in myself," he said, "and when I lose faith, I can't write. It's discouraging. What would you do?"

I told him that his thinking seemed to have turned everything around backwards. Faith doesn't have to come first, it can come later. In fact, faith is not always necessary. Just write. Write badly if you have to, but just write. Forget about faith in your writing. It is no big deal. Faith will be your afterglow; it is not something you need up front.

Victims become passive when they can't find faith, or confidence, or courage to do something. Then they tell themselves they *don't have the power* to do it.

Owners know that faith and courage only appear later in reflection. Action comes first. Action comes before the courage to act. Faith and courage are rewards—not requirements—for action. The power to do something often shows up halfway into the doing of the thing, *not up front*.

"Do the thing," said Ralph Waldo Emerson, "and you shall have the power."

I was living life backwards

I know this sequence for courage because most of my life had been wasted waiting for the power to show up. Or the faith. Or the courage. I thought I had to have it up front before I could act. Before I could be bold. But I had the whole process of this power reversed. Had I not awakened and seen the light, I'd still be waiting to this day for the faith.

"If a thing is worth doing," said G.K. Chesterton, "it's worth doing badly."

The action itself is the source of courage. *Doing it* is what erases the fear of doing it.

I once told my coach Steve Hardison, in an admiring voice, "You can do things other people are afraid to do." He acknowledged that that was true. But he then said, "And the only reason I can do these things is because I have done them. Doing them is how I learned to do them."

In working with corporations' salespeople over the years, I have noticed that there is one thing that motivates a salesperson more than anything else. It's something that is so motivating that it fills a salesperson with almost unstoppable confidence and energy. What is it? It is *making a sale*.

After having made a sale, a salesperson is more confident and energetic than at any other time. Unfortunately, there is a tendency to squander the energy in celebration of the sale instead of *using it* to immediately face the sales challenge they fear the most.

"How can I motivate myself to sell more?" a salesperson asks.

"By making a sale," I reply.

"Well that's just it: I'm too low on motivation to do that. How do I get my motivation level up to where I want it so that I *can* make a sale?"

"Get right into making the sale, and your motivation will go right up where you want it."

That sounds like double-talk to the salesperson. So I often use an exercise metaphor. We are more familiar with this dynamic when it comes to exercise.

"How do I motivate myself to run in the morning?"

"By running in the morning."

"But I don't *feel like* running."

"That's because you're not running yet. If you were running, pretty soon you would feel like running."

Fear is overcome by doing what we fear to do. Action defeats fear, just as scissors cut paper. And paper covers rock, and rock breaks scissors. It's the circle of life. But you've got to start it yourself. It won't happen on its own.

The action you take doesn't even have to be perfect. It will begin to feed itself the power it needs to continue. Like starting a car by pushing it. You start it by *moving*.

Courage has a second wind. Once into it, you'll get more into it. Too much fearful worry prior to the action is the only thing that can stop this process.

When you were a child, you knew this. It was intuitive. You just put your fear in your back pocket and jumped. Remember? At one point, you just pushed off on that bike. At one point, you just jumped off the high board into the deep end of the water. You didn't worry about whether you had what it took to jump. You just jumped.

Somehow, as grown-ups, we have talked ourselves into assuming that we can't do anything we're afraid of doing; that being afraid to do it is the same as being unable to do it. But a little practice at *just doing it* shows us that this was a false assumption. Action generates courage, not the other way around.

Go off by yourself somewhere and sit down with a spiral notebook. (Filmmaker Quentin Tarantino says the spiral notebook is the most high-tech invention of our lifetime because you can take it anywhere, you don't need an electrical outlet or batteries, and you can write *anything* into it.) Write down 10 things you would do in your life if you had absolutely no fear. Then pick one of them to do.

The thing you've picked to do might make you afraid just thinking about it, but that's okay. Don't think about it. Thinking about it is what is making you afraid. Just get started doing it. Without thought.

All courageous people have fear. They just do things anyway, hollering with a combination of joy and fear, like Butch and Sundance jumping off the high cliff into the water below.

You will find, as you descend toward the water, there is a joyful rush. You're feeling your fear *while you are in action conquering it.* And as you continue in action, the fear dissolves, like a fist full of salt in the river. What remains for you is pure joy. It's the joy of being someone you were not. That's reinvention.

You reinvent by doing things "you" wouldn't do, and in so doing you realize there is no fixed and permanent "you" at all.

43

How to Live to Be a Hundred

SOMETHING WEIRD WAS HAPPENING AT the convent!

The nuns there were living longer than they were supposed to, much longer.

The average age of death for women was in the mid-70s, but the nuns at the convent were living an average of 20 years longer than that. Some were in their hundreds!

The convent housed the Sisters of Notre Dame in Mankato, Minnesota, and brain researchers from UCLA believed the nuns had discovered a major secret of long life: the exercise of the human brain. The mother superior in the convent long believed that "an idle mind is the devil's workshop" and so her sisters did not let their minds go idle.

They played mind games such as chess, checkers, and Scrabble. They held seminars and workshops. They wrote to their representatives in congress. They stayed mentally active and actually *increased* their brain activity as they grew in years.

The result was that they didn't die; they lived.

Something happens when the brain takes on challenges. Something beneficial happens to a human being when her brain enjoys and works on problems.

The problem-solving brain grows dendrites (those branches between the cells). And the increase in dendritic growth has been linked by researchers at UCLA to an increase in healthy, active years on the planet.

When the brain is up to something, the body stays alive. When the brain jumps on a problem, the body adds life.

This is why elderly people die so soon after a spouse dies. The other spouse, more often than not, was the sole source of intellectual stimulation, the sole source of "problems" for the mind. So what we used to think of as "problems with the spouse" we now know was giving us life. All problems, providing that they are embraced, are a huge gift.

Why victims die an early death

The irony in this for the victim is that the victim tries to enhance his life by avoiding problems. Even though problem-solving looks like it is the *source* of a long and happy life, victims spend their days trying to find a "hassle-free" existence. They want security above all things. They want a comfortable life. They don't want to have to think about it.

They especially want to have an easy time of it intellectually. Many victims say, upon leaving high school, or college, or whatever their last level of education, "I'm never going to open another book again in my life!" They slam their books down and, with a wicked gleam in their eyes, they set out for a life of mindless comfort. They've *had it* with challenging the mind. They just want to watch TV for the rest of their lives—let their favorite football team live *for* them. Let the cast of *Seinfeld* come up with clever solutions to life's problems *for* them. Let the news talk show hosts, in their sophisticated, cynical way, explain why nothing they do makes a difference anyway.

The things that victims avoid the most—problems—are the very things that would give them more life. If they learned to engage. If they learned to enjoy.

As we saw before, Denmark is one of the most "comfortable" welfare states the world has ever had. In Denmark, the government has set about to take care of everyone's potential problems. *And they have the highest suicide rate in the world.*

In my bathroom at home, I have posted a quotation by William J. Locke. It's there so I can remind myself of it every morning as I start the day:

> I believe that half
> the unhappiness in life
> comes from people
> being afraid to go
> straight at things.

Find something you have been avoiding. A creditor to communicate with. A relative to make an apology to. A person at work you've been meaning to have a heart-to-heart meeting with. Then do it. Go straight at it! Jump into the deep river like Butch and Sundance, without a huge amount of worrying ahead of time. After you've felt the joy that comes with such an action, vow to go straight at something else tomorrow. Soon you'll come to enjoy and respect the life you are inventing.

44

Every Solution Has a Problem

THE PROBLEM WITH PROBLEMS IS our use of the word. Because the word "problem" triggers such a negative shock to our system, the automatic response to it is: "I don't want to think about it." So we call in a consultant. We call in a counselor or a therapist.

The only reason consultants are so good is because they *enjoy* the fact that we have a problem. Because they enjoy it, they can bring enthusiasm and creative thinking to the problem.

I once had the pleasure of working with one of the top political consultants of all time, Joe Shumate. He was brilliant. The value he brought to every campaign he worked on was his love of creative thinking.

While his candidates would become emotionally involved in their campaign's problems, Joe Shumate had no such entanglements. He was there to think. He was there to use his imagination and then to consult.

"The job of a consultant," he once told me, "is to borrow his client's watch to tell him what time it is."

I found this little joke to be very profound. The reason the client can't tell what time it is is because he's not thinking, he's feeling. He's too emotional to read his own watch. He doesn't have a thinking process going on in his head, he has problems.

One of the *real* problems in our society today is the word "problem." We have invested so many decades of fear and loathing into that word that it has now become very hard to even think about our problems positively, proactively, creatively.

So much negative weight has been given to the word "problem" that we now use it as the ultimate word to describe people whose lives are really messed up.

"How's John doing?" I might ask you.

"Not so well," you say.

"Really?"

"Yeah, he's got problems."

"That's too bad. He was a really nice guy."

By demonizing the word "problem," we have hindered our ability to grow and expand. We have robbed ourselves of one of life's greatest joys: problem-solving.

Problems are adventures in disguise

In fact, problem-solving is *such* a joy that companies have to remove it from their office computers. Most companies have taken the computer games off the systems in the office because they are so addictive that employees do nothing but play them.

But these games are just problems in disguise!

We enjoy the problem of how to take the Mario Brothers to another level because we call it a game, not a problem. We enjoy solving the computer game Myst more than our own life's identical journey because we think of Myst as a game.

When I had Tetris and Solitaire on my office computer many years ago, I became so hooked on the games that I had to purge them. Games are problems in disguise. They have simply been translated into a playful, positive language: playing games!

People buy books of crossword puzzles at the magazine stands. But what if instead the books were called "Crossword Problems"? No one would buy them.

In the mall, there is a video arcade with all kinds of electronic games to play. If the sign said "Video Problem Room," no one would go in.

But the truth is, problems are always potentially fun. They are always an adventure in disguise. And they will be that way unless we add fear into the equation. Unless we take them down the ladder. Unless we personalize them.

For example, why is it that we love to hear about *other people's* problems? Surely not because we like other people to be in distress. But rather, because we love solving problems, period. And when they are other people's, we have no fear. Once we take away the fear, we can joyfully jump into problems. That's why we like mysteries, gossip, computer games, and so on. If a friend comes over because he has a problem and he wants my advice, I might secretly enjoy the experience, although I will tell him I'm troubled and concerned for him.

Learn to commit an assault

Voltaire said that no problem could withstand the assault of sustained thinking. And he was right. No problem can.

In my workshops on problem-solving when I present Voltaire's declaration that "no problem can withstand the assault of sustained thinking," I like to ask the participants if they disagree with the quotation. No one ever convincingly disagrees because no one has ever checked out the premise! They don't know what it's like to bring sustained thinking to their problems. Their typical response to a problem has always been, "I don't want to think about it."

If a problem *can* withstand the assault of sustained thinking, then it's probably not a problem.

Sometimes taking a break from sustained thinking and going for a walk will solve a problem even faster. When the mind settles down, intuition comes in and answers appear.

Remember, the ownership position is: If there's no solution, there's no problem. If there's no solution, what we're dealing with is a *fact of life* that we haven't yet accepted. Every problem has a solution, whether we can see it yet or not. And every solution requires a problem. Solutions are fun, but to get one, you need a problem. So what's wrong with problems?

Fearful worrying is not thinking

When someone tells a victim he needs to talk because "it seems we've got a problem," the victim immediately sinks down into the pit of his stomach. He feels the little butterflies. He's no longer thinking; now he is worried.

Worry is not true thought. Worry is a misuse of the imagination. Worry mimics thinking, but it never accomplishes what thinking accomplishes. No one has ever "worried" a solution into existence. To find a solution, we have to get to a level higher than worry.

Albert Einstein saw this clearly when he said, "The significant problems we face cannot be solved at the same level of
thinking we were at when we created them."

Reinventing yourself requires letting worry be a thing of
the past. You can be concerned, but you can't worry. When
you're concerned about something, you immediately look for
the action you can take. You act on concern. Worry makes you
passive. And neurotic.

Reinventing yourself requires problems. They are the
games you play in this great tournament. The tournament is
called the dance, the dance of life. Each game you win advances
you in the tournament.

45

Stop Being Yourself

REINVENTION OCCURS WHEN WE ARE no longer trying so hard to be ourselves. So does joy. We are happy when we are growing.

Therefore, to really experience joy, we have to do something we aren't accustomed to doing. You don't become joyful doing the same ole same ole. No one does. You become joyful doing the unexpected. This joy comes from expanding who we are, and becoming someone we had not been.

Oprah Winfrey's physical trainer, Bob Greene, said, "When I first met Oprah, I never saw her experience joy." This was in spite of the fact that the woman was as rich and famous as anyone has dared to dream of being.

When he asked her when the last time was that she felt any real joy, she had to think more than eight years back to the days when she was filming *The Color Purple* with Steven Spielberg (and in that movie, acting quite brilliantly, *becoming another person* on screen).

Since that time, she had experienced "little bouts of happiness," but no real joy.

Oprah Winfrey was actually fortunate to have *The Color Purple* as a memory. Most people have to think all the way back to their childhoods to recall some real shout-out-loud joy.

But then Bob Greene began to work with Oprah to show her that joy was available to her any place, any time, if she knew how to get to it.

In his book written with Oprah, *Make the Connection*, he describes how the joyful moments began to occur again for her, and how "her strongest joyful moment I ever witnessed came in October 1994. We had been running for over two hours in the pouring rain during the Marine Corps Marathon in Washington, D.C. I looked up and saw the 25-mile marker. It was clear she would finish. I turned around and I saw tears in her eyes."

She had surprised herself. She had become someone she had not been before. She had grown.

In that moment, Greene thought back to when he first met Oprah Winfrey. She weighed 237 pounds and she couldn't look him in the eye. She had made quite a journey since then.

Children know where joy comes from

Kids know where to go to get that feeling of joy. They are constantly trying to do things they have never done.

The famous cry of "Look Ma, no hands!" is a cry of joy, because the child wasn't satisfied with just riding the bike. Then the same child tries riding it with hands up in the air, and the thrill is right there. There is no more joyful cry than when you hear a child yelling, "I did it! I did it!"

It's *doing things* that brings a child joy. As grown-ups, we have forgotten that. We somehow think that it's *feeling things* that will lead to our happiness. Then we start to think it's other people making us feel things that will make us happy. Bad idea, because we've lost touch with what we once knew. We've disconnected from the spirit.

As grown-ups, we can even program the possibility for joy out of our lives by constantly seeking a "hassle-free" existence. By always wanting to find a comfort zone. By constantly looking for "security" instead of something that will challenge us and make us grow. Finding security is like settling on a permanent personality to live inside.

Look, Ma. No joy!

Ask yourself the big question

When we live as victims, we are always seeking to get into a groove or a rut. It is the rut of comfort. We forget that the only difference between a rut and a grave is a few feet in depth.

Meanwhile, although we're stuck in the rut of comfort, our spirit is pacing around inside us like a dog whimpering and aching to go outside and run. The whimpering is sad to hear, and most of us can't stand the sound of it, so we cover it up quickly with food, or adult beverages, or smoking, or television. Or all of those at once!

But the whimpering continues down in the soul. We can still hear it far away, down long hallways in dreams too sad and dark to remember. We might someday know that this beautiful dog that's whimpering is the voice of our own spiritual dyslexia, the God (dog spelled backwards) within longing to express itself. The *en theos* that the word enthusiasm comes from. Longing to go out and run.

Most Americans have been programmed to repeat the question, "How can I get more comfortable?" over and over all day long in their heads.

But not the reinventing you. Not if you are reinventing yourself. Because then, you are different. You have committed to making the connection to joy, like you did as a child. You will always ask yourself, What could I do today that I know would take a lot of glorious effort?

You are going to finish a number of your days with the observation, "It was hard, but it was fun."

46

The Virus Is in Your Biocomputer

THE IMAGES AND SOUNDS WE put into our brains will never leave. They just get filed deeper, to influence us forever.

Every moment we spend on Earth is important. Every 60-second TV commercial we watch is 60 seconds of our lives never to be recaptured. It is 60 seconds we could have spent sending a long-lost friend a postcard. It might have been the postcard that saved their sanity.

I scroll through the movies on my TV that are available to watch. I'm about to make a choice. The choice I make is between a movie that makes me laugh and one that makes me shake my head in disgust. It is a choice that will change my life forever. I pretend it's no big deal.

Pausing after phone calls, I see I have time to make one last call before returning home. My work is finished, so I can call anyone. One friend always cheers me up and shows me life's funniest side. My decision to call him is one of the most important decisions I'll make. Laughter heals and gives added life.

Norman Cousins's book about the literal healing power of laughter, *Anatomy of an Illness,* proved once and for all the powerful effect of laughter and humor on the living cells of the body. We play to an audience of cells.

There are things that make me laugh. There are things that make me sing. There are things that make me get up and dance with happiness. These are the things I want to be most aware of in my life. I want to always have them around me and know where to go to get more.

There is music that makes me shout, "Yes!" and clap my hands as I drive to work. That's the music I want at my fingertips at all times.

I want to pay attention to what feeds my spirit. I want to have my spirit be so important to me that any increase in its activity gets noticed, and noted and remembered for future reference. I want to really get it that I can only reinvent myself by accessing this spirit and letting it stretch me from within.

Please, no more silly love songs

Watching the movie *Jerry Maguire,* I felt my spirit lift as the soundtrack played an old Paul McCartney song from his first solo album, *McCartney.* The song was called "Momma Miss America" and it had raw energy and beauty, and was mercifully free of McCartney's depressingly silly post-Lennon lyrics. After I saw the movie, I bought the soundtrack and played that same track during a break at one of my larger seminars. I watched as the music lifted 400 people the same way it lifted me in the theater. I was glad I paid attention. Some things touch the spirit, and I want to keep knowing exactly what they are.

In my experience, nothing kills the spirit faster than the evening news. The local evening news is worse than national evening news, but not by much. One reason the local TV news is worse is because, these days, the anchors are models, not journalists, and their intelligence reflects that difference. In addition to that, they joke with each other in insincere ways that make the viewer reconsider the whole idea of human life. Sandwiched between the insincere joking is a mission to bring us the most sickening and spirit-killing news they can find. Their entire goal is to make us gasp in horror. It's a proven ratings-booster each time we do.

It is little wonder that Dr. Andrew Weil at the University of Arizona has gotten great results treating his patients with a "news fast." His patients' physical symptoms actually get better if they go for three weeks without watching the evening news. They sleep better, and by doing so, restore health and energy to their cells. The brain doesn't have so many grotesque pictures of mutilation and violence to deal with throughout the night.

Victims gape credulously night after night at the so-called "news" and falsely conclude that the world is getting worse and worse. They increase their fear and secret longing to hide.

Despite the horrible events of 9/11, it is a fact that overall air safety continues to improve. And even though air travel gets safer and safer with each passing month, victims are more and more afraid to travel because they've been watching the same bodies and wreckage being pulled from the same ocean from the same plane that went down weeks ago. They're watching each night as new relatives are found to interview and better, more audio-enhanced recordings of the black box are found to play with subtitles so we can hear the captain and crew.

Television stations have found that ratings will climb when the TV shows appeal to our lowest levels of consciousness. But that's not hard to understand. We usually watch TV when we are tired. (It is rare that we shout out, "I'm feeling full of energy right now; turn the TV on!")

Even the esteemed gonzo journalist Dr. Hunter S. Thompson has observed that "the TV business is a cruel and shallow money trench, a short plastic hallway where pimps and thieves run free and good men die like dogs." That pretty much sums it up.

Reading Dr. Thompson's conclusions reminded me of a remarkable interview I saw on TV a few years ago with Charles Manson from prison. The occasion was the release of Geraldo Rivera's kiss-and-tell autobiography, eloquently titled *Exposing Myself,* in which the talk-show host brags about the variety of sexual "conquests" he has made in his life. In the same book, Rivera also talks about a famous interview he had done with the serial killer Manson shortly after Manson had been convicted of the Sharon Tate murders.

The reason Manson wanted time on TV now was to distance himself from Rivera and his book. He said that Rivera had exaggerated their relationship in his autobiography, and that he, Charlie Manson, didn't want the world to think that he really knew the man that well.

I stopped and thought about that. Here was a notorious, convicted multiple murderer who was more worried about being associated with Geraldo Rivera than he was about his crimes. The murders he could somehow explain and live down. An association with Geraldo Rivera, never.

Take inner responsibility for the things you watch and listen to. You will start to realize more and more that what you watch, read, and listen to has a major impact on your spirit.

Once you flip on the news and become unhappy for a few moments, you will understand clearly and consciously that *you made yourself* unhappy with your own choice of what to watch. The news itself didn't make you unhappy. The on–off button is all yours. You own it. Soon you can take back control of it, and when you do, you'll be on your way to total control of how you program your mind. How you program your mind is what will reinvent who you are.

47

Aren't They Just Grinning Idiots?

IN THE BROADWAY MUSICAL *South Pacific*, one of the most popular songs was about a "cockeyed optimist" who was "immature and incurably green . . . stuck like a dope on a thing called hope."

It illustrates that the culture we live in does not have a very high opinion of optimism. We think of optimism as not being very realistic. When we think of optimists, we think of happy idiots and smiling fools.

We think of the clueless blonde acting all ditzy and happy. We think of Barbie. We think of a Pollyanna refusing to see reality. We think of Mr. Rogers or Richard Simmons. We think of someone running his family into debt by always pretending that good times are just around the corner.

But we are wrong to think this, because optimism is not weak; it is powerful. There's proof.

Twenty years of breakthrough studies by Dr. Martin Seligman show that optimism is realistic and effective. In fact, the optimist is far more tough-minded than the pessimist, because the optimist always *chooses* his or her thinking after reviewing many possibilities, whereas the pessimist hardly thinks at all. In fact, the pessimist is most characterized by *quitting* at the beginning of the thinking process and caving in to a fatiguing sense of defeat.

In *The Optimist Child,* Seligman reveals the results of his scientifically validated studies on more than half a million subjects: "Pessimistic people do worse than optimistic people in three ways: First, they get depressed much more often. Second, they achieve less at school, on the job, and on the playing field—much less than their talents would suggest. Third, their physical health is worse than that of optimists. So holding a pessimistic theory of the world may be the mark of sophistication, but it is a costly one."

Dr. Seligman's studies were a dramatic rejection of the old idea that we have permanent personalities caused by genetics and environment. Dr. Jonas Salk, the inventor of the polio vaccine, told Seligman he wished he had his life to live over. "If I were a young scientist today," said Dr. Salk, "I would still do immunization. But instead of immunizing kids physically, I'd do it your way. I'd immunize them psychologically."

Stop asking how it makes you *feel*

Psychotherapist Alan Loy McGinnis also traces the source of optimism to our thoughts, not our personalities.

"It is our thoughts that cause us so many problems," says McGinnis in *The Power of Optimism.* "We psychotherapists should stop asking our patients, 'How does that make you feel?' and start asking, 'What are the thoughts that make you feel this way?'"

We have absolute control over our thoughts, even though that control often feels difficult. Victims are so close to their thoughts and feelings that they have no sense of control whatsoever. Victims, internally, feel out of control. By feeling out of control, it feels like outside circumstances are causing our negative feelings, just as it *felt like* the Earth was flat for so many years.

The owner's real leverage in life is in whether she or he exercises optimistic or pessimistic thinking responses.

Archimedes said, "Give me a lever long enough and I will move the world," and he was literally correct, that if you had given him a long enough lever, he could have, by a movement of his hand, tilted the entire planet Earth off its axis.

The language we use in our minds and in our conversations is the leverage we've been looking for.

The most famous example of the difference between optimism and pessimism is whether the glass is half full or half empty. Let's say I am dying of thirst in the desert, and you bring me a glass of water filled up halfway. If I am an optimist I'll say, "Thanks for the water!" If I am a pessimist I will say, "Where's the rest of the water?"

So, was the glass *really* half full or half empty? It isn't a matter of which is true, because both perceptions are equally true. It's a matter of which perception is more useful.

When I say the glass is half full, all the cells in my body are listening in. My cells always respond to all my thoughts and my speaking. When I say the word "full," they respond in a more satisfied and biologically grateful way.

It is of more service to my life to be optimistic. It is stronger to be optimistic, and it leads to higher levels of energy.

Talking Back to Prozac

If I complain about the empty part of the glass, my vitality sags with my words. I am disappointed, and the disappointment causes my energy to leak a little. The negative cycle has begun, and it always encompasses mind, body, and spirit.

Dr. McGinnis cites studies that show that optimists excel in school, have better health, make more money, establish long and happy marriages, stay connected to their children, and even live longer.

An optimist is different from a pessimist in this primary way: He or she is *aware of the choice*. There are two ways to see everything: the bright side and the dark side. If I see the choice, I own the outcome. If I don't see the choice, I am a trapped victim.

Even something as "bad" as depression contains a choice. Psychiatrist Peter Breggin, who wrote the courageous *Talking Back to Prozac*, sees something bright in the darkest depression in his patients. "The depth of their depression reflects the heat of passion burning within them. I explain, 'The intensity of your suffering reflects the intensity of your life energy; imagine how fully you will live when you learn to use it creatively.'"

Begin today to study your own habitual way of describing situations. When you see that you've taken a pessimistic view, don't condemn yourself or take the absurd position that it's part of your permanent personality. Simply become interested in it. Then experiment with it. Ask yourself, "What might be good about this situation? How could this situation make me stronger?"

By looking at your life situations this way, you will start to experience a new excitement about your own mind. You will begin to see that your mind was given to you to *use* to create the person you want to be.

48

Feeding the Fire of the Spirit in You

THE HUMAN SPIRIT, LIKE A campfire, must be lit again each day.

Unlike the spirit, a campfire is easy to observe and understand, because we can step back from it and see it. After a night of camping, we can emerge from our tents the next morning and notice with satisfaction that the campfire has gone out. We don't curse the campfire for going out, and we don't think life is unfair because we have to start another fire again the next night.

Yet we don't have that same simple understanding of the spirit. We are confused by the human spirit. We think there is something wrong with a universe in which the spirit must be renewed each day. We don't see the gift in that, because we don't see that the spirit is just like a fire.

It is good that the campfire must be relit because it gives you control over the fire. You can start it or you can pour water over it and put it out. When you realize that you have that same kind of control over the human spirit, you will know how to live. I'm not saying you will be happy forever, but you will always *know how* to be.

And *knowing that you know* will make all your experiences of "unhappiness" feel temporary and inconsequential. Being unhappy will never be a big deal again because you'll experience it the same way you experience "being tired."

Once the spirit catches and is going strong, it feels even more like a fire in that it consumes almost everything in its path and it turns everything else into its own nature. You've seen fire in a forest do that, and you've seen the human spirit do that, too. When truly excited leaders are inspired and aflame with passion for a cause, their enthusiasm is so contagious that the people around them catch the feeling. They catch fire.

When he was asked to give a definition of leadership, Field General Bernard Montgomery said, "The leader must have infectious optimism. The final test of a leader is the feeling you have when you leave their presence after a conference. Have you a feeling of uplift and confidence?"

Once the spirit is really blazing, it consumes everything and everyone with a feeling of uplift and confidence. And it's all an invention, not in the sense of being fake, but in the sense of being real, just like the lightbulb that Edison invented was real. The spirited person you invent yourself to be is just as real, and can just as easily be turned on as Edison's lightbulb.

After each meeting and conversation you have in your personal and professional life, ask yourself whether the person you just met with left feeling higher or lower. Are they further up or down their ladder as a result of meeting with you? Once you have formed this habit, you'll start to shape your conversations accordingly, and people will look forward to being with you. Your spirit will be something they feed on.

Someone sent me an anonymous quote today as I was writing this part of the book. He said it expressed what he felt in a seminar I'd recently given on reinventing yourself: "Help me to believe the truth about myself, no matter how beautiful it may be."

49

Riders on the Storm

WE LOOK THROUGHOUT OUR LIVES for people who will make us happy and light our fires for us. And so we search and search. We sing songs that say "Come on, baby, light my fire."

But we search in vain, because the fire can only start on the inside, not the outside. We've looked outside of ourselves prematurely, searching for help. We need to learn to break back into our prison of solitude, because it's not really a prison, it's a power station. It's where the switch is thrown. It's where the atom is split.

The mistake we have made is to believe we need to "break on through" to something further outside ourselves to find happiness. The further outside, the better! The longing to make that breakthrough is reflected in much of our most intriguing music, such as the music of Jim Morrison and The Doors.

In *The Leveling Wind*, George Will makes a telling observation about The Doors: "Jim Morrison's short, shabby life, and its peculiar echo today, express a longing that waxes and wanes like a low-grade infection but never quite disappears from temperate, rational, bourgeois societies. It reflects a vague—very vague—desire to (in the words of The Doors's anthem) 'break on through to the other side.' Through what? To what? Don't ask. The Doors didn't. People who talk like The Doors are not, as such people say, 'into details.'"

But I think we *do* know the details.

The haunting and poetic music of The Doors—which I still love to listen to—expresses our belief that happiness must be *out there*, on the other side of wherever we are. Somewhere over the rainbow. There's a place for us. Somewhere.

Many sad and beautiful songs like those of The Doors are a version of the dream that "someday my prince will come."

The longing is for someone to take our journey to the spirit *for us*. We keep dreaming about some magic place where the living will be done for us. But the kingdom of heaven is not beyond a star or waiting in some future land. The kingdom of heaven is within us, as a teacher who gave seminars many years ago taught. To think it is *not* within us is a tragic illusion that causes us to waste our lives turning mere humans into idols who can't deliver.

Deepak Chopra quotes an anonymous ancient Indian sage who expressed this tragic illusion perfectly when he said, "All your suffering is caused by a single superstition: You believe that you live in the world, when, in truth, the world lives in you."

Can we really perceive, in a way that's clean and clear, how much the world lives inside *us*?

The Doors took their name from a William Blake passage about "the doors of perception." But it's also obvious that they didn't fully understand the meaning of Blake's famous words: "If the doors of perception were cleansed, everything would appear to man as it is, infinite."

Clean your own perception

The doors of perception are inside our own minds. They are not out there. The job of cleaning is an inside job.

You can notice each and every filthy victim's thought you think. You can listen to yourself speak and notice when you are being cynical for no reason. You can study the link between fatigue and pessimism and learn ways to get your energy up.

You can experience first-hand the wisdom in Gandhi's advice to "*be* the change you wish to see in others." You can learn to notice when you are trying to get happiness for yourself by changing others. You can learn to replace that thinking with more creative thinking. You can learn to clean out *everything* that muddies up your perception and stops you from seeing the infinite possibilities of life. You can invent someone amazing if you want to.

50

Finding the Love
Behind the Mask

COLIN WILSON REFERS TO THIS continuous personality expansion of reinventing yourself as "spiritual metamorphosis."

In fact, Wilson says, in his *Anatomy of Human Greatness*, "the refusal to keep repeating the act of spiritual metamorphosis is the reason that all great artists cease to develop."

Like Picasso, who regressed into immaturity in his later paintings. Like Elvis Presley, who took his journey backward. Like Dylan Thomas, who crawled back into the womb of alcohol. Like Kurt Cobain, who tried to match heroin, his living death, with suicide, the more permanent form of the same thing.

Behind the death mask of human personality there is a life force dying to express itself and be happy. It's the child's natural love of life.

Amy Tan's powerful novel *The Joy Luck Club* was based on a real-life group of women. Her mother's friends used to get together each month to play mah-jongg. "The Joy Luck Club" was what they called their group. The women knew they needed joy and excitement in their lives, and they *knew they were in charge of creating it.* So they built it into their routine in the form of a fun and unpredictable game. They made their own joy and luck happen.

In our teen years, we unconsciously make a death mask to wear. It is shaped from our embarrassments, real and imagined. Then we call the mask our personality.

The mask hides the love of life we had as children. That love is all we had, and now we've hidden it, and covered it up so the air can't get in. Personalities are not fun, vibrant things; they are what we crawl inside of to die.

Freedom from this death mask is found in enthusiasm and excitement. It is found in spirited self-creation, inspired by a project, a purpose, or a game we have decided is worth winning. (In games we find our lost love of life.)

If we will become aware of the possibilities of ever-expanding self-invention, we can then look to express a self that surprises us a little more each time, a self not yet fully realized or habituated, like Oprah in *The Color Purple* or Oprah running the marathon in the rain.

My friend Kate is a good example of reinventing yourself. When I first met her, there were a lot of things she was afraid to do, including being assertive and speaking in a public setting. Most people would have just written that off as a part of their personality. "I'm shy in public," they would say, endearing themselves to their own weakness. But Kate has been a proponent of personality-busting from the moment she found out that she could do it.

Today, she is winning awards at Dale Carnegie for her improvisational speaking. Most people never would have signed up to learn how to do what they feared doing. Kate was committed to reinventing herself upward every chance she got. She now works out in a gym every day simply because she didn't like "who she was" physically. So she changed who she was. It is the greatest-kept secret of modern life that we can do that.

We don't have to do it in huge ways, either. Sometimes, the smaller the better. Tiny personality changes here and there inspire growth in us constantly. Inspiration leads to enthusiasm.

When Emerson said, "Nothing great was ever created without enthusiasm," he wasn't just talking about works of art, he was talking about individual lives. No one creates a great life without reconnecting to the enthusiasm experienced in childhood.

And anyone can make that connection. Any time. It has nothing to do with age. (In fact, people often use the aging process as a cover story to hide their avoidance of this effort.) It has nothing to do with circumstance. And it does not depend on other people. The spirit is in us already. It is the love behind the mask.

51

The Human Spirit's Secret Weapon

MAKE A DECISION TODAY TO take possession of the most powerful weapon there is in the battle against a sad life. That weapon is called "practice."

And it seems to be a total secret to 90 percent of America! Pick it up and you'll give yourself what feels like an unfair advantage over everyone else you know.

Academy Award winner Anthony Hopkins uses this secret when he "over-rehearses." In preparation for the movie *Nixon*—his greatest challenge as an actor—he rehearsed each scene more than 100 times before shooting it.

I know great salespeople who "over-prepare" in the same way. They learn so much about a sales prospect's business that the prospect wants to make the salesperson a partner after their first meeting. Selling becomes easy. It becomes almost irrelevant compared to the shared enthusiasm of the two people.

Legendary trial lawyer Gerry Spence talks about how he developed his mesmerizing voice through singing and loud rehearsals in his car driving to work in the morning. Spence would rehearse the expression of various emotions, booming his voice through the interior of his car. When he spoke in the courtroom, everyone sat up and took notice. If the opposing attorney had a bland, monotonous voice, it was because he didn't know about the secret of practice. The opposing attorney probably thought his weak voice was a part of his personality. He probably thought his opponent, Spence, was born with a "gift."

The gift was practice.

When the old San Francisco 49ers were finished with a practice session, one player stayed on the field. He would ask one of the backup quarterbacks to stay with him to throw him passes. That player was Jerry Rice, the best pass receiver of all time. By practicing more than anyone else in professional football, Jerry Rice went into each game knowing he had a secret advantage. There is no faster route to self-confidence and self-esteem than to use that secret advantage.

Sweet Judy blue eyes

Many years ago when I was a slovenly counterculture hippie rebel beatnik student, I used to hang out at a little coffee house in Tucson, Arizona, called Ash Alley. There was a little-known folksinger who sang there on occasion, and I loved to hear her sing. One night, someone in the audience requested a song and she declined to sing it, although she said she knew it. She told the audience that she never performed a song until she had sung it 200 times in private, making it her own. The singer's name was Judy Collins. At the time I saw her song-ownership idea as a charming ritual. I was too hip at the time to realize that she was talking about practice.

Jack Twyman was an NBA star who had the odd habit of arriving early at practice and shooting the ball exactly 200 times before real practice began. Sportswriters used to call him one of the greatest "pure shooters" the game had ever seen. By "pure" they meant that his smooth, accurate shots flowed from him "naturally," as if he were born shooting. They didn't know his secret. His shooting was made pure through practice.

As a young boy, I became fascinated with the musical *Peter Pan*. I think I identified with Peter's bold commitment not to grow up. One day, my mother read an article aloud to me about Mary Martin, the actress who starred in that Broadway play. Mary Martin used to practice for her big parts in Broadway musicals by putting on boxing gloves and pounding the big bag while singing at the top of her lungs. By singing the songs over and over while hitting the punching bag, she developed an awesome vocal power. Once she could sing her songs while pummeling the bag, they became effortless on stage.

In the era before sophisticated microphones were used in plays, Mary Martin was known for her ability to fill a huge theater with her voice. How did this tiny woman, the critics asked, inherit such an enormous voice?

It wasn't inherited. It was the result of practice.

It was not genetic.

There is no gene for the human spirit.

God is alive. Magic is afoot. This I
mean to whisper to my mind. This I
mean to laugh within my mind. This
I mean my mind to serve till service is
but Magic moving through the world,
and mind itself is Magic coursing
through the flesh, and flesh itself is
Magic dancing on a clock, and time
itself the Magic Length of God.

—Leonard Cohen
Beautiful Losers

RECOMMENDED BOOKS

Dauten, Dale. *The Max Strategy*. New York: William Morrow & Company, 1996.

Glasser, William. *Choice Theory*. New York: Perennial, 1999.

Goldberg, Jason. *Prison Break*.

Goss, Tracy. *The Last Word In Power*. New York: Currency, 1995.

Katie, Byron. *Loving What Is*.

Neill, Michael. *The Inside Out Revolution*.

Seligman, Martin. *Learned Optimism*.

Welsh, Sherry. *Slowing Down*.

Wilson, Colin. *The Essential Colin Wilson*. Berkeley, Calif.: Celestial Arts, 1986.

———. *Frankenstein's Castle*. Bath, England: Ashgrove Press Ltd., 1982.

———. *Beyond The Occult*. New York: Carroll & Graf Publishers, 1989.

INDEX